Inclusion

Other titles in the No-Nonsense series:

Steps in Leadership
Huw Thomas
1 84312 434 3

Inspection and Accountability
Bill Laar
1 84312 436 X

Managing Finance, Premises and Health & Safety
David Miller, John Plant and Paul Scaife
1 84312 454 8

Making the Most of Your Headship
Gerald Haigh and Anne Perry
1 84312 435 1

Inclusion

Linda Evans

Routledge
Taylor & Francis Group

LONDON AND NEW YORK

First published 2007 by Routledge

2 Park Square, Milton Park, Abingdon, Oxon, OX14 4RN

Simultaneously published in the USA and Canada by Routledge

270 Madison Ave, New York, NY 10016

Routledge is an imprint of the Taylor & Francis Group, an informa business

© 2007 Linda Evans

Typeset in AdobeGaramond by RefineCatch Ltd, Bungay, Suffolk

Printed and bound in Great Britain by MPG Books Ltd, Bodmin

Note: The right of Linda Evans to be identified as the author of this work has been asserted by her in accordance with the Copyright, Designs and Patents Act 1988.

British Library Cataloguing in Publication Data
A catalogue record for this book is available from the British Library

Library of Congress Cataloging in Publication Data
Evans, Linda, 1951 Oct. 3-
Inclusion / Linda Evans.
p. cm.
Includes bibliographical references.
ISBN-13: 978-1-84312-453-5 (pbk. : alk. paper)
ISBN-10: 1-84312-453-X (pbk. : alk. paper) 1. Inclusive education—Great Britain—Handbooks, manuals, etc. 2. Special education—Great Britain—Handbooks, manuals, etc. I. Title.
LC1203.G7E86 2007
371.95′2—dc22
2006032647

ISBN 10: 1 84312 453 X

ISBN 13: 978 1 84312 453 5

Contents

Foreword

There are many adults around, undoubtedly including lots of school governors, and perhaps a few teachers, who remember when the word 'ineducable' wasn't an exasperated insult but a long-standing, supposedly neutral, technical term applied to, among others, every single child with Down's syndrome. That changed only in 1971 with the putting into effect of the groundbreaking 1970 Education Act that removed the 'ineducable' label from over thirty thousand children. In that year - and it's really not so long ago - for the first time in our history every single child won the right to go to school.

Even then, of course, it was assumed that for many children 'normal' schooling (that word was commonly used) was inappropriate. That assumption held sway in official policy for virtually the remainder of the twentieth century. The significance of that, and the importance of Linda's book, lie in the fact that anyone who's been teaching for a long time – and in the natural order of things, this includes most of those in positions of leadership – will have had their methods and approaches formed at a time when schooling was divided into 'mainstream' and 'special' sectors, each inhabiting its own world of professionalism and career development.

The predictable result is that in this area, as in so many others, official policy runs well ahead of practice on the ground. All the way down the line, from government legislation, through school policy documents to classroom planning sheets, brave intentions are undermined by assumptions and attitudes that simply, with the best will in the world, haven't caught up. Linda quotes Ofsted, in 2004,

> *SENcos in almost half of the primary and secondary schools*
> *visited identified the perceptions of staff as a major barrier to*
> *effective inclusion.*

Small wonder, then, that the staffroom cry of 'he shouldn't be in this school at all – he needs specialist attention!' is not only still frequently heard, but it is difficult to challenge, given the way that schools conventionally are organised, and the collective mind-set of the communities which they serve and which have an influential share in their governance.

Special educational needs, let's not forget, is only one aspect of inclusion, which is actually an all-embracing term intended to cover all children who are at some risk of being put at a disadvantage in our school system. For convenience we think of these children in categories – Linda lists nine. Some are immediately recognisable – 'pupils belonging to minority ethnic and faith groups', 'gifted and talented pupils'. Others call for a moment's thought before we realise just how valid they are – 'young carers' for example. These categories are necessary if we're to tackle the issues, and Linda deals with them methodically and with great practical insight.

The truth, though, is that the categories overlap and interact in a host of different ways. So, as Linda emphasises, we should always be looking at the child and his or her individual needs, and not at the labels, which can be inadequate or misleading. Official recognition of this comes in the government's drive for 'Personalised Learning' and, of course, the *Every Child Matters* agenda. (That great friend of children in trouble Camilla Batmanghelidj, who runs Kids Company in London, speaks of 'Turning *Every Child Matters* around, and looking instead at "what matters to every child".')

All of that, of course doesn't just seem daunting to the head or classroom teacher. It actually is a considerable challenge. Running an inclusive school is difficult and can at times be confrontational. (Linda describes the way that emotions can run high in staff meetings when it comes to discussing provision for a child who is taxing a teacher's professionalism and patience.)

As an author, though, Linda's great strength is that she writes for us with an authority founded in deep and extensive practical experience.

Her advice on how to set up a 'Circle of Friends' to help a child whose behaviour is challenging is just one example of how she provides direct help to concerned teachers.

In one of her many concise passages of advice, Linda suggests that in a truly inclusive learning environment a child can feel free to take risks, make mistakes and be unafraid to ask for advice. My immediate reaction was to think that applies equally well to teachers. If they're going to build that inclusive classroom, they too will have to take the risks and make the mistakes. They'll need to ask for advice, too, and in that regard, this book by Linda Evans makes an excellent starting point.

Gerald Haigh
January 2007

Acknowledgments

My thanks to: colleague and friend, Tina Collins, not only for giving me valuable feedback on my manuscript, but also for giving me insight over the years into the heart and mind of a conscientious and caring head teacher; David, my husband and 'critical friend' for his encouragement, scrupulous checking of text, and ability to keep calm in the face of technological crisis; to head teacher Matthew Oakley and deputy head teacher Zoe Welsh for sharing their 'pupil swap' experiences with me – their enthusiasm and dedication is the stuff that true 'inclusion' is made of; last but not least, Theresa Best, of Routledge, for her patience and valuable guidance.

Chapter 1

What does inclusion mean?

In this chapter we will consider:

- ■ what inclusion means to different people;
- ■ official definitions;
- ■ developing a shared understanding of inclusion in your school.

What does inclusion mean? The answer to this question may seem obvious, but ask around – you'll get lots of different answers. Most head teachers will be familiar with the relevant Ofsted speak by now, but definitions offered by teachers, support staff and parents will be many and various.

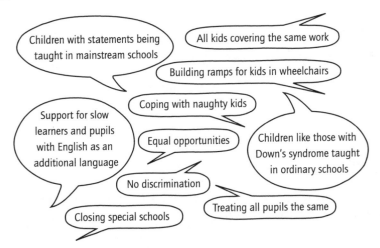

Children with statements being taught in mainstream schools

All kids covering the same work

Building ramps for kids in wheelchairs

Coping with naughty kids

Support for slow learners and pupils with English as an additional language

Equal opportunities

Children like those with Down's syndrome taught in ordinary schools

No discrimination

Closing special schools

Treating all pupils the same

Inclusion has been a major thrust of the Government's education policy in recent years and permeates all official documentation. In coming to a meaningful definition of what inclusion means in your own school, it may be useful to re-visit some of the 'official' interpretations.

■ Some official definitions of inclusion

DfES

At the time of writing, the Government's policy is driven by the *Every Child Matters* agenda and emphasises schools' responsibilities in including children with a diversity of additional needs, both within and beyond the school learning community. It aims to reduce educational failure and maximise potential for all children. The promotion of full-service extended schools supports inclusion, contributes to children's holistic development and removes barriers to achievement.

> *Inclusion is about the quality of children's experience; how they are helped to learn, achieve and participate fully in the life of the school.*
> (DfES, Removing Barriers to Achievement 2004a)

The National Curriculum

The National Curriculum sets out the statutory requirments that schools must follow in terms of providing *effective learning opportunities for all pupils based on their cultural, physical and learning needs*. It established three principles for developing an inclusive curriculum:

1 setting suitable learning challenges;

2 responding to pupils' diverse learning needs;

3 overcoming potential barriers to learning and assessment for individuals and groups of pupils.

Ofsted

Inspectors are tasked with evaluating a school's performance in terms of 'inclusion' in spite of this often being at odds with the main areas of focus, i.e. performance in terms of pupil achievement (SATs scores) and value for money.

> *An educationally inclusive school is one in which the teaching and learning, achievements, attitudes and well-being of every young person matter. Effective schools are educationally inclusive schools. This shows not only in their performance, but also in their ethos and their willingness to offer new opportunities to pupils who may have experienced difficulties.*

(Ofsted 2000)

CSIE and the Index for Inclusion

The Centre for Studies on Inclusive Education (CSIE) is an independent body working in the UK and overseas to promote inclusion and is funded by donations from trusts, foundations and grants. In the late 1990s, the centre produced and trialled the *Index for Inclusion*, a set of materials to guide schools through a process of inclusive school development. This work was financially supported by the DfEE, including free distribution of the Index to all primary, secondary and special schools and LEAs in England.

The view of inclusion in the Index is a broad one and includes:

- valuing all students and staff equally;

- increasing the participation of students in, and reducing their exclusion from, the cultures, curricula and communities of local schools;

- restructuring the cultures, policies and practices in schools so that they respond to the diversity of students in the locality;

- reducing barriers to learning and participation for all students, not only those with impairments or those who are categorised as 'having special educational needs';

- learning from attempts to overcome barriers to the access and participation of particular students to make changes for the benefit of students more widely;

- viewing the difference between students as resources to support learning, rather than as problems to be overcome;

- acknowledging the right of students to an education in their locality;

- improving schools for staff as well as for students;

- emphasising the role of schools in building community and developing values, as well as in increasing achievement;

- fostering mutually sustaining relationships between schools and communities;

- recognising that inclusion in education is one aspect of inclusion in society.

The Code of Practice for Special Educational Needs and the SEN and Disability Act (2001)

A large part of the inclusion agenda revolves around provision for children with specal educational needs and/or disability. The two most important pieces of guidance/legislation to impact directly on these areas are the Code of Practice for Special Educational Needs (SEN) (DfES 2001b) and the Special Educational Needs and Disability Act 2001 (SENDA).

Both pieces of guidance/legislation emphasise children's rights to be educated in mainstream settings, with the onus on schools to make appropriate provision (see Chapter 2 for more detail).

Developing a shared understanding of inclusion

The first step is to agree upon a definition that makes sense to your particular school, its staff and children, which everyone can 'buy in to'. This will determine the ethos underpinning everything that contributes to building and running a learning community.

Agreeing a definition will require discussion and honest exploration of people's feelings and experiences. Be prepared for emotion. I have been in more than one meeting where opinions have clashed. In one, a year 4 teacher (the mother of a child with Down's syndrome being taught in a mainstream school – after a hard fight with the local authority) almost came to blows with the year 6 teacher who was struggling to cope with a difficult class and felt strongly that one particular pupil could be better catered for in a special school. For the first teacher, mainstream schooling had become synonymous with human rights; she believed passionately that her son needed to be amongst his neighbourhood friends at school if he was to grow up being accepted by the local community. She had transferred this passion to the debate about the (entirely different) pupil in year 6. The second teacher saw that one individual was disrupting the education of a whole class and felt he needed expert intervention.

It's important that these views are aired, because otherwise resentment can bubble away beneath the surface and do no end of harm. If there is opposition to inclusion, it often stems from a teacher's lack of confidence in her ability to cope. 'I already work all the hours God sends to do my best for the little blighters, how can I plan a whole different load of stuff for some kid who can't read or write? It's just too much.'

SENcos in almost half the primary and secondary schools visited, identified the perceptions of staff as a major barrier to effective inclusion.

(Ofsted 2004)

Some starting points

Inclusion is about looking out for those individuals who, for whatever reason, may find themselves left out or overlooked, unable to participate in the activities – social and academic – that are usually associated with school. For a minority (usually those whose behaviour interferes with the learning of others), an official exclusion may result; for the majority of minorities (if you see what I mean), the 'exclusion' may be more subtle but just as damaging. It may take the form of feeling isolated from peers by too much withdrawal from the classroom; being 'velcroed' to a support assistant so that other children keep their distance; being shunned by peers (and teachers) because they don't know how to talk with you/help you/understand you; feeling left out because you are 'different'; feeling too scared to do anything because you are being bullied; feeling a failure because you never succeed at anything.

Identifying those children 'at risk' in this sense is a major task for any school but, for now, step one is to come up with a definition of inclusive practice that will be at the heart of the school's mission statement. Some starting points are provided below.

> *Inclusion is . . . about the quality of each individual's experiences in school, in terms of learning certainly, but also in terms of being respected for who they are.*

> *Inclusion is . . . recognising different types of gifts and abilities and providing opportunities for everyone to succeed (everyone is good at something).*

> *Inclusion is . . . identifying individual learning needs and providing for them.*

> *Inclusion is . . . the creation of a learning environment where barriers to learning are avoided wherever possible.*

You'll notice that that I have used 'individual' rather than child or pupil in the first definition, because if a school is truly inclusive, all of these principles apply just as much to the adults involved – teachers, assistants, lunchtime supervisors, parents and governors. This must be a case of 'do what I do' rather than 'do as I say' and, as a senior manager, you must lead by example.

So, if Mrs Baker is hard of hearing, be sure to speak clearly, sit on her 'good side' and look at her so that she can see your lips moving. Recognise that your staff, just like your pupils, will have different learning styles; so be ready to use visual prompts when explaining something at a staff meeting, ask questions to check understanding and test opinions, and allow for thinking time. Get to know your staff as individuals, their fears, strengths and limitations. Give praise for good work and useful suggestions and give credit wherever it's due. A short, handwritten note of thanks will mean a lot to the recipient and be a powerful 'reinforcer'. Refrain from criticising staff and acknowledge all contributions, no matter how small. (For help with recognising different types of personality among your staff, and effectively supporting/cultivating them, see *Steps in Leadership*, also in this series (Thomas 2006).

What inclusion is *not*

Inclusion is not a matter of making tokenistic gestures . . . for example, buying in some specialist software but not getting it networked and not getting staff trained in how to use it to good effect with pupils who need it.

It's not a matter of just ticking the box. 'Yes, we have a teacher with a specialist qualification from the British Dyslexia Association (BDA) (unfortunately she is not able to work with Freddie Smith because he's in a different class to three other children who need her help).' 'Yes, all staff have had a half day's training on special educational needs (but in fact the adviser ran out of time and so we never got on to thinking about the half a dozen children we have with autistic tendencies).'

It's not about treating everyone the same. Equality of opportunity is not a case of giving all pupils the *same* opportunities but rather enabling them to fulfil their potential – in a variety of ways, by means of providing *appropriate* opportunities. Additional work outside the classroom ('withdrawal') is a case in point – and another area where people can get emotional. They can see it as stigmatising and somehow punitive, denying children the shared experience of class activites.

But one-to-one or small group teaching can be an excellent way of accelerating progress and boosting a child's self-esteem. It allows for more intensive, carefully matched work than can be achieved in a class of thirty. Situations have to be handled sensitively of course, but in a school that celebrates diversity and accepts people for *who* they are rather than for *what* they can do, there shouldn't be resistance to any type of effective differentiation. The key is in making sure that all kinds of children experience some sort of 'tutor time', whether this is for literacy 'catch-up', mentoring, playing a musical instrument or as part of a 'gifted and talented' programme.

You're probably thinking, 'Good idea, but what about staffng?' The frequency of these sessions can be different according to need, and tutors may be teachers, teaching assistants, senior staff, mentors (including volunteers from the community, student teachers and pupils from a nearby secondary school) – as long as they have appropriate 'training'.

Where pupils are withdrawn from class, make sure that the following issues have been addressed:

- give it a positive name, for example 'tutor time';

- sessions should be planned and evaluated jointly (class teacher plus the person delivering the training);

- the 'tutor' should have appropriate training and skills;

- timing is important – avoid a pupil missing a subject they are good at and/or enjoy;

- link the work to what is happening in the class as far as possible;

- allocate a proper space – not a cloakroom or a stretch of draughty corridor;

- manage the child's return to the classroom – invite them to share what they have been doing and explain what others have done while they were out of the room.

Recognising different groups of vulnerable children

Inclusion is about equal opportunities for all pupils, whatever their age, gender, ethnicity, attainment and background. In a large inner-city school where all the pupils are of Asian descent, the one white child may be vulnerable in terms of being accepted by the other children; similarly, the child with a strong Geordie accent will be the 'odd one out' in a small rural school in Cornwall and the little girl from a family of travelling hop-pickers may well be ostracised in a class of well-to-do home counties children.

There is potential for each and every one of us to feel 'left out' at some time or other in our lives. Gender is another factor. Teachers can, quite unwittingly, favour boys or girls in their class, possibly reflecting the gender of their own children. Pupils who are gifted and talented can also have a rough ride. They may hide their ability to avoid being a target for bullies, which can lead to significant underachievement.

Chapter 2 looks at the children who are most likely to be vulnerable in terms of not being included.

Chapter 2

Who are the children at risk?

In this chapter we will consider:

■ different groups of 'vulnerable' children;

■ some of the issues for your school.

Any child who is 'different' from others in the peer group is potentially vulnerable in terms of not being included. There are a number of groups who may be particularly at risk, including:

■ pupils belonging to minority ethnic and faith groups;

■ travellers and gypsies;

■ asylum seekers and refugees;

■ pupils who need support to learn English as an additional language (EAL);

■ pupils with special educational needs;

■ gifted and talented pupils;

■ children in public care;

■ children with medical conditions;

■ young carers;

- children from families under stress;

- pregnant schoolgirls (a very small number in primary schools);

- pupils who are at risk of disaffection and exclusion.

You need to know which of your pupils belong to these various groups, what their particular needs are, and how to make good provision for them. You should also be vigilant in monitoring their progress and development.

This chapter provides some information about different groups and outlines some of the issues associated with them, acknowledging, however, that each sub-group, and each individual within those sub-groups, will have unique personal circumstances.

Minority ethnic groups

These include:

- different ethnic and faith groups;

- travellers and gypsies;

- asylum seekers and refugees;

- pupils who need support to learn English as an additional language.

Pupils with different skin tones, different languages and different faith systems and cultures are a fast-growing group in many areas. In some schools, these pupils may in fact be the majority group and enjoy an environment where diversity is not only accepted but actively celebrated. In other settings, however, pupils – and their parents – may need a steer in accepting families from countries and/or backgrounds different from their own.

The importance of multicultural and anti-racist education cannot be overstated: it must be one of the most crucial functions of schools in the twenty-first century. Awareness, tolerance and developing understanding must run through the whole curriculum if we hope to promote a society that values diversity. This means that rather than pretending we are 'all the same', we have to acknowledge and sometimes celebrate differences, not least in the visual images displayed around the school. Pupils need to see themselves and their own culture reflected in photographs and posters, books and other media in order to create a positive impression of the way they eat, dress, think and talk.

> *The [Macpherson] report does not place a responsibility on someone else; it places a responsibility on each of us. We must make racial equality a reality. The vision is clear: we must create a society in which every individual, regardless of colour, creed or race, has the same opportunities and respect as his or her neighbour.*
>
> Jack Straw (The Home Secretary) speaking on the publication of *The Stephen Lawrence Inquiry* (the Macpherson report), February 1999.

A report published shortly after the Lawrence Inquiry (Ofsted 1999) suggested that most local education authorities and schools lacked clarity and direction when it came to addressing inequalities of attainment between different ethnic groups. The report observed that:

> *Although most schools have equal opportunities policies, few have clear procedures for monitoring their implementation and their impact on practice is limited.*
>
> (Ofsted 1999: 7)

British culture

British culture is multi-ethnic, and has been since Roman times. After World War II, migration to Britain led to the establishment of communities of non-white minority ethnic groups which, in 1991, comprised 7 per cent of the UK population. According to Labour Force Survey figures, by 1995 about 50 per cent of the minority ethnic population had been born in the UK.

The term 'multicultural education' has in some instances, become synonymous with a type of education that is aimed at black and minority ethnic pupils (rather than one that *includes* these pupils). But the white population also contains different ethnic groups, such as Welsh, Irish and Scots, as well as immigrant populations from European countries.

The perspectives from these assorted cultures should be included in teaching cultural diversity. Care should also be taken to avoid representing black and minority ethnic cultures in terms of stereotypical artefacts, traditions and customs (for example, equating steel bands with West Indian culture; saris and samosas with Indian culture). Although it is important for pupils to understand where cultures and religions come from, they also need to know that cultures undergo change, both in their lands of origin and in new homelands. For example, in the UK, black, British and British Asian youth cultures have emerged that are distinct from their parents'.

Remember, too, the children of mixed heritage (approximately one in twenty pre-school children in Britain is of mixed heritage). Such children's needs and experiences must be considered, with sensitive handling in cases where there might be tension over the dominant culture.

Children who are newly arrived from overseas may have specific needs. It is important to know about their cultural and religious background in order to be able to make them feel safe and able to join in with class activities. (The Qualifications and Curriculum Authority website contains comprehensive information about countries of origin, cultural background, religions practised and languages spoken: www.qca.org.uk.)

It is also useful to remember the importance of basic human requirements as reflected in the Every Child Matters (ECM) outcomes 'being healthy and staying safe' (DfES 2003). If physiological needs are not being met, for example getting enough to eat, it is unlikely that a child will be 'fit for learning'. Liaison with other agencies may be essential to ensure that appropriate arrangements are in place for the child's family (and to avoid sad scenarios like the child stealing food from the bird table to take home for hungry parents and siblings).

Children from asylum seeking and refugee families offer particular challenges to schools. They may have been forced to leave their homes in order to escape war and persecution; they or members of their family may have been imprisoned, abused and tortured; they may have seen loved ones being killed. Not surprisingly, these children are often psychologically and emotionally disturbed by the traumatic experiences they have undergone and in need of mental health support.

Information about and support for asylum seeking families

Action for Children in Conflict (AfC) provides psychological, emotional and educational support to the survivors of conflict. Trained key workers provide a climate of support and befriending tailored to the needs of young people and their communities (www.actionchildren.org).

The Home Office produces reports on the countries that generate the largest number of asylum applications in the UK under the following headings:

- background information;

- languages, ethnicity and culture;

- religion;

- the education system in the home country;

- some issues for teachers and schools in the UK;

- useful resources.

Information is also available at www.refugeecouncil.org.uk.

Disaggregating the overlapping needs of these pupils can be extremely difficult, and distinguishing between learning difficulties, emotional instability and English as a additional language needs requires carefully planned, step-by-step assessment. First steps might include:

- finding out about skills and knowledge already acquired (an interpreter/family member/community worker may be needed);

- making available some culturally familiar resources;

- careful engineering of acceptance into the class;

- teaching other children about the child's home country and culture, developing positive images;

- presenting learning tasks that are meaningful and achievable;

- allowing the child to respond in their own way;

- being patient and devoting time and energy to the development of social interaction with, and by, the child.

Pupils with special educational needs

The Code of Practice for Special Educational Needs identifies four main areas of special educational needs.

- cognition and learning needs;

- behaviour, emotional and social development needs;

- communication and interaction needs;

- sensory and/or physical needs.

As all teachers know, individual children do not always fit neatly into boxes, and in many cases may experience difficulties from more than one category. A child with Down's syndrome, for example, may well have learning difficulties and a hearing impairment, which have an impact on their ability to communicate. These various difficulties often result in uncooperative behaviour.

The important thing is to identify the barriers to learning – whether they stem from the child, the learning environment or (most likely) the interface of both. If a child has a short attention span, for example, this may not present any problem at home, where they can run about freely and choose what they want to do – and for how long. It only becomes a problem when they start school and find that they are expected to sit on the carpet and listen to the teacher for what, to them, seems a very long time.

Early identification and effective intervention is the key. This is not to ascribe a particular label to a child, but to put into place, as early as possible, strategies for support. A reasonable settling-in period should be followed by careful evaluation of a child's needs and identification of any barriers to learning. An important aspect of this, but one that is often overlooked, is consulting with parents for their views on the child's needs. And, of course, it is important to involve the child as well. Where a child goes on to School Action Plus, and possibly formal assessment resulting in a statement, the record of steps taken by the school will provide valuable information.

The Foundation Stage Profile provides detailed baseline information on children as they progress though the reception year, but initial work can be started very early on in nursery using a simplified (albeit quite crude) assessment tool such as an early years basic checklist (see Figure 2.1).

This checklist was in fact used by one school to evaluate the impact of its mothers and toddlers group – the scoring enabled staff to compare children who had attended the group, with those who hadn't. The checklist doesn't have to be used like this of course; it can be adapted to suit your specific needs.

A valuable spin-off of using something like this with parents is that it indicates to them the sort of developmental steps that are important. Parent, child and teacher sat down together to complete the checklist and the child drew a picture as part of the assessment; staff were able to 'casually' suggest ways in which parents could play with their children at home to stimulate them and practise early skills. If you can set up a proactive intervention like this one, your staff will not only be establishing good relationships with parents and carers, but also helping to give children a good start as early as possible in their education – and avoid them becoming one of the 'vulnerable'.

Mainstream schools are increasingly expected to provide for children with significant learning, communication and behavioural difficulties. The successful inclusion of these children calls for a school-wide awareness and understanding of diverse needs and an acceptance that, on the whole, children are not 'being awkward on purpose'. They want to succeed; they want to fit in; they want to please. But they may not know how. Schools need to build up a wide repertoire of strategies and resources to meet this diversity of needs – and train staff on how to use them to best effect (more on this in Chapter 3).

Name:		DoB:		
Recording achievement: 0 = never; 1 = just beginning; 2 = sometimes; 3 = usually.		Date	Date	Date
Social	1 Plays with another child in cooperative activity.			
	2 Shares toys.			
	3 Responds to requests for help.			
	4 Waits for turn (e.g. on slide).			
	5 Can take off and put on coat.			
Language	6 Listens to a story for five minutes.			
	7 Speaks in sentences: 'I want that. I like ice-cream.'			
	8 Joins in reciting a nursery rhyme.			
	9 Answers a simple question: 'Where is. . .?'			
Motor	10 Holds a pencil correctly.			
	11 Draws a picture/pattern.			
	12 Copies a simple shape.			
Pre-reading/numeracy	13 Shows an interest in books.			
	14 Turns pages properly.			
	15 Can point to details in a picture.			
	16 Recognises own name in print.			
	17 Recognises and names colours.			
	18 Counts 1–5 in imitation.			
	19 Counts five objects.			
	20 Recognises numerals 1–5.			

Figure 2.1   Early years basic skills checklist

▪ Children with disabilities

For children whose disability is physical and/or sensory, with or without significant learning difficulties, the issue for the school is one of access – both to facilities and curriculum/extra-curricular activities. There is now legislation protecting any child who is substantially affected by their disability in one or more of the eight areas listed below:

- mobility;

- manual dexterity;

- physical coordination;

- ability to lift, carry, move objects;

- continence;

- speech, hearing, sight;

- memory, ability to learn, concentrate, understand;

- impaired perception of risk or physical danger.

It is unlawful for schools to discriminate against these pupils for a reason relating to their disability, and the Disability Discrimination Act 2005 requires schools to promote equality of opportunity for disabled people by making 'reasonable adjustments' to the learning environment and planning to increase access over time.

Reasonable adjustments

Schools need to respond to the Disability Discrimination Act legislation by making adjustments to their policies and practices as well as looking carefully at a child's individual needs. When deciding if a reasonable adjustment is necessary, think about the pupil being disadvantaged in terms of:

- time, effort and inconvenience needed to achieve something that may be instant and easy for others;

- indignity or discomfort incurred by not having proper facilities/equipment;

- loss of opportunity, academically and socially;

- diminished progress in life skills, curriculum knowledge and understanding, and cognitive functioning.

If a child is in a position where any of these situations arise, the school may be seen at fault.

What is a reasonable adjustment?

(a) choosing an accessible venue for a school trip;

(b) using a sounding ball for football;

(c) demolishing the school and rebuilding on one level;

(d) swapping round classrooms;

(e) setting up a buddy system;

(f) providing a laptop;

(g) planning lessons so that all children make progress.

Answer: All are reasonable adjustments except (c) (too expensive and impractical) and (g) (already an entitlement).

This is a whole school issue and all staff, teaching and non-teaching, and governors should be involved in the formulation and regular reviewing of the school's accessibility plan.

To make reasonable adjustments schools will need to:

■ **Plan ahead**: just because you have no children with, for example, visual impairment this year, it doesn't mean that you won't have next year. Re-decoration/refurbishment, new building and re-designation of rooms should include consideration of children (and staff) with mobility and sensory difficulties. Consider how colour can be used to best effect; use white edging on stairs and counter tops; use different floor coverings to signal different areas, fit blinds at windows to eliminate glare.

■ **Identify potential barriers**: this can make an excellent project for year 6 pupils. Let them try to get around the school in a wheelchair, identifying where ramps may be needed, doors widened, etc. In some respects, the physical barriers are the easiest to identify and overcome (even if sometimes costly); it is the less tangible issues of curriculum access that can be more tricky.

■ **Work collaboratively with disabled pupils, their parents and other agencies**: talk to parents – they have often found solutions to problems at home that can be equally effective in school. Seek the advice of staff from the local authority's sensory support/mobility services. Invite a disabled person into school to help with the audit.

- **Identify practical solutions through a problem solving approach**: a lift may be a good solution, but impossible to implement in the near future. How, then, can you solve the problem of Peter in year 4 who now needs to use a wheelchair, when the year 4 classroom is on the first floor? This is not too difficult! You will obviously re-locate the year 4 base, just as you might if the year 4 teacher was suffering from bad arthritis. If the information technology suite is on the upper floor, though, you will have to be imaginative in ensuring that Peter has access to technology, perhaps with a small group of friends, in a ground floor location. If the library is on the upper floor, a ground floor mini-library could be established, or at least a good selection of books in boxes should be brought down to the classroom.

- **Ensure that staff have the necessary skills**: continuing professional development (CPD) is an essential requisite in making good provision for pupils with significant impairments. Make use of outreach services offered by local special schools, or contact voluntary organisations for advice on practical aids and strategies that really work. Simple techniques can go a long way to meeting children's needs – for example always looking at a child with hearing impairment when you speak; using signing to support what you say; use visual timetables; place some displays at eye-level for wheelchair users; enlarge worksheets to A3 size for visually impaired children. Where a teaching assistant or care assistant is allocated to a specific child, they should obviously have the necessary skills in handling the child, administering medication, etc.; sharing these with other staff will also be valuable.

- **Monitor the effects of adjustments on a pupil's progress**: start by asking them how things are. When/where are the difficulties? What works well, not so well?

You will know that you have succeeded in making reasonable adjustments when disabled pupils are participating fully in school life (and after-school activities), both in the classroom and outside, and staff feel confident about meeting their needs.

■ Gifted and talented pupils

The Department for Education and Skills (DfES) in its Excellence in Cities programme defined *gifted* pupils as the most academically able in a school. This ability might be general, or specific to a particular subject area such as mathematics. *Talented* pupils are those with high ability or potential in art, music, performing arts or sport. The two groups together form 5–10 per cent of the school population, but are not, of course, uniformly distributed. Pupil populations differ greatly and children considered very able in one setting may not stand out in another, but it is important for schools to recognise the 'most able' within their setting and ensure that their needs are met.

Whatever the general level of ability within a school, there has been a tendency to plan and provide for the middle range, to modify for those who are struggling and to leave the most able to 'get on with it'. This has meant that some of the most able pupils have:

■ not been challenged and stimulated;

■ under-achieved;

■ not had high ambitions and aspirations;

■ become disaffected.

It is generally recognised that schools that make good provision for this group are good 'high performing' schools generally. They accept that the most able pupils may have particular needs and are as deserving of additional support and planning as are their less able peers. They cultivate a 'cool to be clever' ethos in school, where high achievement is celebrated alongside more modest achievement and no child is ever afraid to be 'the best'. They also recognise, however, that children who are gifted and/or talented may have difficulties – perhaps with social skills and lack of emotional maturity; perhaps they are dyslexic or have problems with coordination. Careful evaluation of the needs of gifted and talented pupils is just as important as consideration of children with special educational needs.

Identifying gifted and talented children is the first step in making good provision for them. Many will, of course, identify themselves. They are the precociously able who always know the answers, are fascinated by their favourite subject, come up with new ideas and new ways of doing things. They may not stand out so well, however, if they have untidy handwriting, are dyslexic, or lack confidence and speak hesitatingly. Those from families where education is not highly valued may also be less conspicuous, as may children who speak English as their second (third or fourth) language.

Children with high ability will usually be easy to spot if they are given the appropriate opportunities to 'shine'. This means creating a school where opportunities are as rich and varied as possible – using outside providers if necessary to bring in expertise, linking with other schools, theatres, sports academies, etc. A child may have the makings of a world-class swimmer, but if they never get to go to a swimming pool, they are not likely to develop the innate aptitude they may have.

Identification will involve a portfolio of evidence including:

- different forms of quantitative and qualitative data (test scores, SAT scores, performance assessments, sports certificates, etc.);

- information from parents (they may be biased, but they also know their child better than anyone else – listen to them and reach your own conclusions); teachers – current and from previous schools; other children;

- samples of work.

The most important part of accurate identification is providing a challenging and supportive environment where children have opportunities to demonstrate any, and all, kinds of ability. This needs to be coupled with a continuous process of 'talent spotting' where teachers and other staff are constantly on the look out for glimpses of genius. Some pupils will be easy to identify at a very early age, while others will emerge later.

Lesson planning needs to be flexible if teachers are to meet the needs of their most able children, with opportunities for depth and breadth to be built in at the planning stage, rather than having to 'think on their feet' when a child finishes in ten minutes what everyone else takes half an hour to do.

Breadth (sometimes called 'enrichment') involves additional experiences/activities/materials and can result in a more complete understanding of the focus area. It enables pupils to compare and contrast, to locate their learning in a wider context and to make connections between different areas of learning, using and applying skills in different situations. Breadth can also include learning a completely new subject, such as Latin, perhaps in an after-school club.

In adding breadth to the curriculum, however, there is inevitably a risk of overload. Be guided by pupils' interest and curiosity and don't expect them to work harder and longer than other children.

Depth (sometimes called extension) is achieved by asking children to delve deeper into a given subject or topic and may come as a result of working closely on one text, problem or artefact. It may involve learning new facts, concepts or skills. Another way of introducing depth is to bring experts into the classroom; this will be of interest to the whole class, but perhaps some time could be spent with the most able children, developing high level skills or exploring more advanced concepts.

Pace refers to covering the curriculum at a faster rate and can result in exceptional achievement for the age range. This is sometimes termed 'acceleration' and involves pupils moving ahead of their peers in the formal curriculum, often working at higher levels in one specific area. Joining a class of older children, or attending a neighbouring secondary school for some lessons, are ways of facilitating this type of progress. Able children enjoy learning alongside others of similar intellectual ability, and it's important that they are given this sort of opportunity.

Tasks for the most able pupils should be about HOTS (Higher Order Thinking Skills), not MOTS (More Of The Same) and should include:

■ analysis, synthesis and evaluation;

■ consideration of difficult questions;

■ reflection;

■ problem solving and enquiry;

- exploration of diverse viewpoints;

- formulation of opinions;

- connections between past and present learning;

- independent thinking and learning.

Teachers use a number of strategies for effectively differentiating work in the classroom. These include providing all children with a common task that invites different responses and outcomes; tasks that vary in difficulty (as in graded exercises) so that able children can begin at an appropriate level and progress further, or different tasks linked to a common theme.

Activities designed to challenge the most able children will tend to be open ended, moving them from concrete to abstract thinking, simple to complex situations, and require a greater level of independent thinking and working. This is not to suggest, however, that these pupils should be 'left to get on with it'. They like to talk with teachers and other adults, try out their theories and discuss possibilities. They also need encouragement and support, just like all the other children. If motivation becomes a problem and teachers feel that a child is 'coasting', individual targets or 'challenges' can be useful in helping to 'stretch' pupils and involving them more in their own learning.

Where children are seen to be talented in sport or in creative/performing art, a school may find it more difficult to provide appropriate opportunities for development. In these cases, think about other local schools and colleges, sports clubs, theatres and orchestras and find out what they could offer a child who has high potential.

National Academy for Gifted and Talented Youth (NAGTY)

The new awareness of the issues surrounding gifted and talented education has resulted in the setting up of NAGTY, with a remit to provide information and training for teachers, as well as opportunities outside school for the most able pupils (www.nagty.ac.uk).

■ Other pupils who are at risk of disaffection and exclusion

Sick children

Children who cannot attend school because of injury or illness can feel very isolated from friends and 'the real world'. Schools can do a lot to counteract this by keeping up regular communication by letter, cards, email and telephone, as well as visiting. Providing work as and when the child is well enough to cope will also help to minimise problems of catching up on return to school – another issue to be considered. Where the child has a home or hospital tutor, school needs to be in close contact, helping to plan work, monitoring progress and providing suitable resources.

Information and communications technology (ICT) plays an increasingly important part in out-of-school education. New technology is already allowing some children with medical needs to access their own virtual school. Using a computer can vastly improve access to learning at home, and in hospital, with CD-ROMs, email and the Internet being used to good effect. It is also a speedy and effective way of sending homework during a short period of absence.

On return to school, the child may need special support in building up strength and stamina and may need to be given medication. Contact with parents, and possibly with the supervising medic/physiotherapist, can help in planning effective support.

Schools should:

- have a policy and a named person responsible for dealing with pupils who are unable to attend school because of medical needs;

- notify the local authority/education welfare officer if a pupil is, or is likely to be, away from school due to medical needs for more than fifteen working days;

- supply the appropriate education provider with information about a pupil's capabilities, educational progress, and programmes of work;

■ be active in the monitoring of progress and in the reintegration into school, liaising with other agencies as necessary;

■ ensure that pupils who are unable to attend school because of medical needs are kept informed about school social events;

■ encourage and facilitate liaison with peers, for example through visits and videos.

See *Access to education for children and young people with medical needs* (DfES 2001c) for more detailed guidance and information.

Medicines in schools

An increasing number of children rely on medication, particularly those diagnosed with asthma. It's important for schools to have clear policies and procedures in place to ensure that the handling and administering of medication is done in way that protects both children and staff.

A policy should cover:

■ procedures for managing prescription medicines that need to be taken during the school day;

■ procedures for managing prescription medicines on trips and outings;

■ a clear statement on the roles and responsibility of staff managing administration of medicines/administering medicines;

■ a clear statement on parental responsibilities in respect of their child's medical needs;

■ the need for prior written agreement from parents for any medicines to be given to a child (for early years settings prior permission is a mandatory requirement);

■ the circumstances in which children may take any non-prescription medicines;

■ the school policy on assisting children with long-term or complex medical needs;

- a policy on children carrying and taking their medicines themselves;

- staff training in dealing with medical needs;

- record keeping;

- safe storage of medicines;

- the school's emergency procedures;

- risk assessment and management procedures.

Managing medicines in schools and early years settings (DfES 2005b) provides advice for schools and their employers on the development of such policies. It also provides general information on the four most common conditions – asthma, diabetes, epilepsy and anaphylaxis.

Children in public care

In March 2004 there were 61,100 children and young people being looked after by English councils, and 4,516 in Wales:

- boys, children from some minority ethnic groups, disabled children and those from lower socio-economic groups are over-represented in care;

- looked-after children are nine times more likely than their peers to have a statement of special needs;

- most unaccompanied asylum-seeker children under 16 are taken into care when they arrive in the UK;

- the majority of looked-after children are in mainstream school.

It is agreed that while children in public care are no more or less able than the general population, their educational success is extremely low. Pupils in public care are thirteen times more likely than other pupils to be excluded from school. SATs scores tend to be low and government figures show that in 2003–04, only 6 per cent were achieving five good GCSEs, compared with around half of all young people: only 1 per cent go on to university.

Several factors contribute to the success of those who have been in care. These include:

- stable and consistent care;

- early reading;

- regular school attendance;

- support from well-informed foster carers;

- having a mentor;

- understanding the importance of education for future life chances;

- financial support for further and higher education.

Every school should have a designated teacher to act on behalf of children in care, monitoring their progress and performance and informing and supporting other staff. Find out what is provided by your local authority in terms of training for designated teachers (for example on the care system; the impact of care on education; statutory responsibilities and associated regulations and guidance).

School governors are responsible for ensuring their schools are not neglecting the welfare and educational needs of children in care in their schools and you should provide them with regular reports on their general progress.

In addition to the usual school records for all children, every child in care must have a personal education plan (PEP), which forms part of the wider care planning. Care plans are reviewed at minimum statutory intervals and progress in education is considered at these reviews. (Local authorities have a duty to promote the educational achievement of looked after children under section 52 of the Children Act 2004 and must ensure that all looked after children have a PEP.)

Different PEP formats are used by different local authorities, but all will:

- set clear objectives for the child, relating to academic achievement and personal and behavioural targets, both in and out of school;

- identify who will be responsible for carrying out the actions agreed in the plan, with timescales for action and review;

- cover the child's achievement record (academic and otherwise);

- identify development needs and set short- and long-term targets.

The school's designated teacher should be involved in agreeing and reviewing a PEP along with the child (according to understanding and ability), the child's parent and/or relevant family member or carer, and the social worker. If a looked after child joins the school without a PEP, the designated teacher should pursue the matter with the child's social worker, who is responsible for initiating it.

A child's PEP is particularly useful at times of transition, whether from primary to secondary school or from one setting to another. It enables information to move quickly with the child, so that they can be placed appropriately and provided with the support and services they need. The child's own thoughts and concerns are an important part of the PEP and a sample template for recording these is shown in Figure 2.2.

Young carers and children from families under stress

A lack of awareness in school is a contributory factor in vulnerable children remaining 'hidden', in spite of the dramatic effect that home circumstances can make on their lives. A significant number of children have to manage without the parental support we would like them to have – for a variety of reasons. These may include looking after a parent or carer who is ill or who is a drug user/alcoholic, or looking after younger siblings while parents are at work. They have to organise their own meals, wash their clothes, get up by themselves in time for school – we can begin to understand how their priorities may not include finishing that geography project for homework!

A child's health is often severely affected due to lack of sleep and the amount of household chores and physical care they undertake. Almost a third of young carers have serious educational problems, falling behind with their work, missing school, or being late for lessons; they can suffer loneliness and isolation, taunting and bullying at school; they are unable to join in with after-school activities and homework is a low priority. Many become truants.

Child: _____   **School:** _____

What do you like most about school?
Can you describe some things that you do really well at school?
Is there anything about school that you worry about?
Is there a teacher or anyone else who really helps you with your education? What is their name?
Who are your best friends?
What are your favourite activities?

Record of achievement success and merit awards etc. (after school clubs, teams, etc.)

Figure 2.2   A template for recording a child's view of school

It is vital that schools identify and support young carers and children from families under stress, making appropriate allowances and offering mentoring, counselling and other therapeutic work.

This chapter has raised issues concerning specific groups of children. In Chapter 3 we consider what an inclusive school looks like – steps you can take concerning overall policy and whole school practice.

Chapter 3
What is an inclusive school like?

In this chapter we will consider:

- leadership and effective inclusion policy;
- appropriate terminology and how people talk about and treat one another;
- the role of SENco and working with other professionals;
- communications.

Leadership

As with most aspects of successful schools, strong leadership is key in establishing inclusive practice. If staff feel that the head teacher and senior managers are merely 'going through the motions' in terms of meeting officially specified criteria, their own practice will follow suit. If you're serious and genuine about being inclusive, your vision for the school will reflect this, your policy will spell it out and your practice should breathe life into both.

- Ensure that the school community feels safe, valued and respected. Reinforce this through displays, newsletters, noticeboards and published information to parents, staff and pupils. You may need to produce this in different languages and formats.

- Ensure the curriculum is inclusive in (a) its content and (b) its accessibility. It effectively addresses issues of diversity, disability, racism and bullying. Opportunities to teach about intolerance, justice and equality should be regularly reviewed.

■ Assemblies should reinforce the school's inclusion policies by being accessible to everyone, tackling issues such as bullying, providing positive role-models (for example speakers from outside school), being interactive.

■ Make sure that the choice of food for lunch/breakfast/breaktimes reflects the range of pupils' tastes and requirements.

■ Ensure there are procedures for addressing prejudice, racism and bullying. Responses to racist bullying should be 'swift, proportionate, discreet, influential and effective' (Ofsted). Never turn a blind eye to an incident, or consider it too insignificant to follow up. Keep a record of all incidents.

■ School performances should include all children in some way (not only the best actors/readers/singers).

■ Make sure your inclusive policy works for parents, visitors, governors and school board members. This includes easy access, appropriate toilets, induction loops in the hall to facilitate hearing; access to interpreters and British Sign Language users.

■ Ensure parents are involved at every level, and empowered. They should know who to contact if they are worried about anything and how to arrange to see them.

■ You should regularly canvas children's views and involve them in finding solutions, through class activities and through structures such as school councils.

■ The governing body should routinely discuss inclusion matters in terms of access, achievement and cases of bullying/racism.

■ Ensure you have good relationships with member of the local community, police, support agencies and voluntary organisations and can work with them to address any tensions beyond the school gates that may impact on school life.

Above all, make sure that you are *approachable, available and askable*. Give pupils, staff and parents enough time to tell you everything they need to. Cultivate the environment of a 'listening school'.

It's not fair

A pupil complained bitterly today about an incident in the playground. 'All right, I'm overweight and I'm not proud of it. But it really gets to me when other kids go on about it. Last week I lost it. I was out of order, right, but when these two kids called me Fatso, and said a whole lot of other things about my size, stupidly I swore at them and used the word Paki. I got done for racism and was excluded for a day and my parents were informed and all, and I'm really pissed off, and nothing at all has happened to the kids who wound me up. It's not fair.'

How should this situation be handled? You could use this scenario and question as a starter activity for a staff meeting or INSET day.

(Amended from www.teachernet.gov.uk)

■ Effective inclusion policies

Most schools make reference to inclusion and/or equal opportunities in their prospectus and promotional brochures, with mention of 'valuing the individual', 'helping every child to succeed', etc. A more detailed equal opportunities/inclusion policy might be designed collaboratively by staff and include the points below:

■ seeking and using pupil and parent perspectives;

■ designing and enacting clear procedures for recording and acting on racist incidents;

■ generating and sustaining an ethos that is open and vigilant, and enables pupils to discuss 'race' issues and share concerns;

■ developing and communicating high expectations, with clear communication that underperformance by any group is unacceptable;

■ reviewing curricular and pastoral approaches to ensure their sensitivity and appropriateness;

■ using ethnic monitoring as a routine and rigorous part of the school's self-evaluation.

The next step is to ensure that this ethos permeates policy throughout the school, not least in the area of teaching and learning.

Teaching and learning: The equal opportunities policy of Perton First School

■ Teachers ensure that the classroom is an inclusive environment in which every pupil feels that their contributions are valued.

■ All pupils have access to the mainstream curriculum.

■ Teaching is responsive to pupils' different learning styles and takes account of different cultural backgrounds and linguistic needs.

■ Teachers take positive steps to include all groups and individuals.

■ Pupil grouping in the classroom is planned and varied. Allocations to teaching groups is kept under continual review and analysed by ethnicity, gender and background.

■ Teaching styles include collaborative learning so that pupils appreciate the value of working together. All pupils are encouraged to question, discuss and collaborate in problem-solving tasks.

■ Teachers encourage children to become independent and to take responsibility for their learning.

■ Teachers challenge stereotypes and foster pupils' critical awareness and concepts of fairness, enabling them to detect bias and challenge inequalities.

■ Resources and displays reflect the experience and background of pupils, promote diversity and challenge stereotypes in all curriculum areas. They are reviewed regularly to ensure that they reflect the inclusive ethos of the school.

■ Appropriate terminology

There is a lot of so-called 'political correctness' around how we talk about people. Concern about saying the wrong thing can have a very negative effect, hampering useful discussion and positive outcomes. I remember sitting in a local authority meeting some years ago, run by a representative of the then Ethnic Minority Support Service. There was so much emphasis on not using the term Afro-Caribbean ('It's a hairstyle, not an ethnic group.') and an insistence that everyone should refer to specific rather than general ethnic groups, that most people were tongue-tied. Nothing useful was achieved, except to make people very nervous.

Some might say that the exact words we use are less important than *how* we use them. But it *is* possible to give offence, quite unwittingly. By establishing some ground rules and leading by example, you can establish appropriate terminology in school. Run a staff meeting or INSET session to develop shared usage and understanding between colleagues, raising awareness of some of the issues with which they may not be familiar.

Remember that language usage changes; what may be acceptable now, could well be 'out of fashion' next year. The activities outlined below may be useful for this sort of discussion. Use them to start off a staff meeting and decide, with staff, on a common vocabulary for your school.

Mind your language: Activity 1

Consider each pair of words or phrases and discuss the differences in meaning and nuance between them.

equality	diversity
racist bullying	racist incident
racially motivated	racially aggravated
religion	faith
Indian sub-continent	South Asia
Gypsy	Traveller

racism	xenophobia
Caucasian	white
Arab	Muslim
West Indian	African-Caribbean
BME people	coloured people
sensitivity	political correctness

Arab/Muslim: Not all Arabs are Muslims and not all Muslims are Arabs.

Minority ethnic/ethnic minority: The term *minority* frequently has connotations of being marginal or less important and in many neighbourhoods, towns and cities in Britain it is mathematically inaccurate. The term *ethnic* on its own is frequently misused as a synonym for 'not-white' or 'not-western', as in phrases such as 'ethnic clothes', 'ethnic restaurants', 'ethnic music'. There is frequently an implication of exotic, primitive, unusual, non-standard. It may be better to use the term 'ethnic group' in a similar way to phrases such as 'religious group', 'linguistic group' or 'national group'.

BME/coloured: The term BME (black and minority ethnic) has come into official use in recent years. It has all the disadvantages of the terms *minority* and *ethnic* mentioned above, but implies that black people are not of a minority ethnic background. The term *coloured* was at one time considered to be polite, but is nowadays widely considered to be offensive.

Mind your language: Activity 2

As a general rule, when you are talking about children with special needs encourage people to 'see the child' before the 'disability':

Not 'the SEN child'	but 'the child with special educational needs'
Not 'the Tourettes boy'	but 'the boy with Tourettes syndrome'

Avoid derogatory terms like thick, moron, lame, subnormal, retarded, afflicted, even in the relative privacy of the staff room. Use terms such as 'learning difficulties' and 'impairment'.

Not 'the spastic girl'   but 'the girl with cerebral palsy'

Not 'the crippled child'   but 'the wheelchair user'

Not 'the handicapped boy'   but 'the boy who is disabled'

Avoid using the term 'normal'; instead, say 'able-bodied' or 'of average ability'.

Naming systems

It is important to use the correct name and style when speaking to someone, as a mark of respect and to avoid confusion and possible embarrassment or offence. Naming systems can differ from culture to culture; understanding them can help people avoid making inaccurate assumptions about personal relationships. For instance, in some Hindu families each person drops the surname and uses their middle name instead, meaning that every person in the family could have a different surname. In the Muslim naming system the order of a person's full name is not fixed or significant, women do not usually change their names upon marriage, children do not necessarily have their father's name and a family might not have a family name.

The safest course of action is to ask people directly how they wish to be addressed. As a matter of courtesy, staff should pronounce names in the same way as a client. When a name is required for official documentation, ask the person:

- what they wish to record as their personal name and family name, for official purposes;

- the order of the name;

- the spelling.

Because some languages place less emphasis on the use of vowels, it may be that the Romanised version of a name will be spelled differently by different people (for example, Latif/Lateef; Surriea/Surya).

For more information, contact your English as an additional language/Ethnic Minorities Achievement Service; there is also useful guidance on the Fife Council government website (www.fife.gov.uk/topics/index.cfm).

Governing bodies and school boards

■ Attach particular governors or school board members to specific groups of vulnerable children so that they can follow those pupils' progress through the school and become a mouthpiece for them, reporting directly to the governing body or school board.

■ Encourage governors and school board members to attend training courses, to promote their own personal development, and enable them to contribute to taking forward school thinking.

■ Governors must know about Disability Discrimination and Racial Equality regulations. Useful information includes:
   – *Accessible Schools*: DfES guidance on disability access (DfES 2002);
   – *Special Educational Needs and Disability in Mainstream Schools: A Governor's Guide* is available from NASEN (Gordon and Williams 2002);
   – The *Disability Rights Commission* website contains a range of codes of practice relating to employment and the responsibilities of schools (www.drc-gb.org);
   – The *Commission for Racial Equality* has a Statutory Code of Practice and explanatory guide on how schools can fulfil their general and specific duties to promote race equality (www.cre.gov.uk).

■ How people talk about and treat one another

Winning the hearts and minds of your staff with regard to inclusion issues can be one of the most difficult things you have to do.

Developing understanding and empathy can be the key – backed up by staff training to increase confidence and ensuring that resources, both human and material, are adequate.

Start in the staffroom. Are staff mutually supportive? Do they share experiences, successes and failures, good ideas, resources? Or is the atmosphere more one of backbiting and sniping, one-upmanship and useful resources in locked cupboards? Does conversation involve discussion of pupils and how they can be supported in their learning, or feature comments like:

> *'You won't get anywhere with him, I taught his brother last year – well, I tried. It was a complete waste of time.'*

> *'You only have to look at their mother to see they're never going to make anything of themselves.'*

> *'What can you expect? Their culture doesn't value learning and doing well at school.'*

It goes without saying that senior managers should always counteract this type of comment, but doing it in a way that doesn't put down the speaker is a real skill.

Some team-building might be called for; opportunities for collaborative problem solving, social get-togethers, shared presentations. These types of occasions could go hand-in-hand with training sessions:

■ Ask the SENco to lead a session about children with communication difficulties in a staff meeting. Invite a speech and language therapist. Simulate what it's like to have difficulties by getting staff to work in pairs:
  – person A doesn't speak any English; person B has to tell him how to get from school to the nearest shop/pub/bus stop;
  – person A wears earphones to reduce hearing capability; person B has to use gesture and other means of communication to explain playtime supervision and how the rota works;
  – person A cannot speak at all and has to use signs and symbols and so on to tell person B what she did at the weekend.
  These simulations may seem simplistic, but they can bring about a real shift in perception. I regularly ask teachers to sit on their

'writing hand' and perform a writing task with the 'wrong hand'. It demonstrates very effectively how laborious writing can be for lots of children, how hard they have to work to write even a short piece and how deflated they feel when they see the untidy/illegible results of their labours. You could also ask someone to wear a pair of sunglasses that have been smeared with Vaseline and then copy something from the board (with everyone else). They feel isolated and demotivated and may begin to understand how it feels to have visual impairment (or even very dirty spectacles!).

- Invite a speaker to talk about their cultural background, special educational need, or what it's like to raise a child with Down's syndrome – whatever is relevant to your own setting. The speaker has to be good. Go on the recommendation of someone you trust, or seek out an opportunity to hear the speaker yourself before booking them. Attending conferences and exhibitions is time consuming but it can be a good way of finding suitable speakers.

- Ask the head of your local special school or unit to host a training session for your staff. This could include a presentation about specialist software/hardware, learning Makaton or using a picture exchange communication system.

- Books are a great way to give staff, and pupils, insight into the lives of people who are 'different'. Order in some appropriate books – make it easy for them. (For a list of recommended books, see Figure 3.1.)

Senior managers as well as all teaching and non-teaching staff should take part in all activities. If some managers and staff use the time for something they see as more pressing or important, the whole exercise will be devalued in the eyes of others.

The role of the SENco

I have suggested above that the SENco lead a session of staff training, and will take this opportunity to emphasise the importance of the

Foundation stage, pre-5 years old and early years	Key stage 1 and P1 to P3	Key stage 2 and P4 to P7	Teachers and other staff
Fiction			
Floppy (1999) Guido Van Genechten (Mantra Publishing Ltd) *Hungry! Hungry! Hungry!* (2000) Malachy Doyle (Andersen Press)	*Boris, the Beetle Who Wouldn't Stay Down* (2000) Hiawyn Oram (Andersen Press)	*Fly, Bessie, Fly* (1998) Lynn Joseph (Simon & Schuster Books) *How the World Began and Other Stories of Creation* (1996) Andrew Matthews (Macdonald Young Books)	*The Curious Incident of the Dog in the Night-time* (2004) Mark Haddon (Vintage). About a boy with Asperger's syndrome. *Lost for Words* (2001) Elizabeth Lutzeier (Macmillan Children's Books). The story of a Bangladeshi girl's first year in London.
The Perfect Little Monster (2000) Judy Hindley (Walker Books) *Skip across the Ocean* (1995) Collected by Floella Benjamin (rhymes) (Francis Lincoln)	*Herb, the Vegetarian Dragon* (1999) Jules Bass (Barefoot Books) *Hue Boy* (1992) Rita Phillips Mitchell (Victor Gollancz Ltd)	*Panda's Puzzle* (1977) Michael Foreman (Hamish Hamilton) *Six Perfectly Different Pigs* (1993) Adrienne Geoghegan (Hazar Publishing Ltd)	*Martian in the Playground* (2000) Clare Sainsbury (Lucky Duck) *My Left Foot* (1990) Christy Brown (Vintage). A writer with cerebral palsy recounts his childhood struggle to learn to read, write, paint and finally type, with the toe of his left foot.
Susan Laughs (1999) Jean Willis (Andersen Press)	*Lily's Secret* (1994) Miko Imai (Walker Books)	*The Visitors Who Came to Stay* (1984) Annalena McAfee (Hamish Hamilton)	*Brick Lane* (2004) Monica Ali (Black Swan). Set in Tower Hamlets, about the life of an Asian immigrant girl. The story deals cogently with issues of love, cultural difference and the human spirit.
	Prince Cinders (1987) Babette Cole (Hamish Hamilton)	*Weslandia* (2000) Paul Fleischman (Walker Books)	*Life, Interrupted: The Memoir of a Nearly Person* (2006) James McConnel (Headline Review). James was finally diagnosed with Tourette's Syndrome and, at long last, began to understand himself.
	Something Else (1994) Kathryn Cave (Viking) *Some Things are Scary* (2000) Florence Parry Heide (Walker Books) *Three Cheers for Tacky* (1996) Helen Lester (Macmillan Children's Books)		
Non-fiction			
	W Is for World (1998) Kathryn Cave (Francis Lincoln Ltd) *Wake Up World!* (1999) (CD-Rom) Beatrice Hollyer (Frances Lincoln Ltd)	*Racism* (1999) Jagdish Gundara and Roger Hewitt (Evans Brothers Ltd) *Voices from Eritrea* (1991) Rachel Warner (ed.) (Minority Rights Group)	*Listen to Me: The Voices of Pupils with Emotional and Behavioural Difficulties* (2000) Susan Wise (Lucky Duck) *ADHD: A Challenging Journey* (2003) Anna Richards (Lucky Duck). A mother provides a fascinating insight into her son's condition.

Figure 3.1 Recommended booklist

SENco role in establishing effective inclusion. The status given to this person will reflect the importance given by the school to the whole concept of meeting individual needs. Believing that it is every teacher's responsibility (which it is) will not guarantee good provision. There has to be someone with a specific remit.

This person may have any of a fast-growing choice of titles (teaching and learning manager, diversity director, inclusion coordinator, curriculum support manager, learning support coordinator) but should always have a high status within the school, empowering them to promote good practice and provide guidance for individual teachers. There should be active support from, and monitoring by, the leadership team. The SENco role is constantly evolving, most recently in the light of *Every Child Matters*, but main responsibilities are outlined below. In many cases, the SENco's workload will preclude them from having a teaching commitment.

> *SENcos play a pivotal role, coordinating provision across the school and linking class and subject teachers with SEN specialists to improve the quality of teaching and learning. We want to see the SENco as a key member of the senior leadership team, able to influence the development of policies for whole school improvement.*
>
> (DfES 2004a: 58)

The Role of the SENco

- To have a strategic view of special educational needs and inclusion throughout the school;
- to oversee an effective system of early identification of needs;
- planning and management of intervention programmes (including Wave 2 and Wave 3);
- development of alternative teaching strategies; ensuring effective differentiation;
- overseeing/planning individual programmes and writing of IEPs;
- management of statutory assessments and associated paperwork and meetings;

- management of additional support staff;
- liaison with parents, external agencies and other specialist staff;
- tracking pupil progress;
- budget/resource management;
- providing CPD for staff, governors and parents.

For more details, see the National Standards for Special Educational Needs Coordinators TTA 1998, available at www.tda.gov.uk/teachers/hottopics/sen/nationalstandards.aspx.

■ Working with other professionals

One of the most important aspects of the SENco role is to establish good working relationships with a range of people outside school. The Every Child Matters agenda and Safeguarding Children guidance makes this imperative. The list can be long:

- speech and language therapists;
- educational psychologists;
- occupational therapists;
- GPs;
- health visitors;
- counsellors;
- community police officers;
- support service personnel (learning support, sensory/physical, traveller service, etc.);
- special school/unit staff;
- social workers;
- education welfare workers;

- parent and volunteer helpers;
- organisations such as CRUSE (bereavement counselling).

Increasingly, schools are pooling funds to employ, for example, a speech and language therapist to work on different sites. This is proving to be a very effective way of accessing specialist knowledge and achieving 'joint working'. Professionals get to know each other and how individual schools work; head teachers feel that this sort of arrangement represents good value for money.

Safeguarding children

The Every Child Matters guidance places a strong emphasis on schools' responsibility to keep children safe, especially those from families living in stressful circumstances. Examples include: families living in poverty; where there is domestic violence; where a parent has a mental illness; where there is drug or alcohol abuse; where a parent has a learning disability; where the family is subject to racism and other forms of social isolation; where the family lives in an area of high crime rates, poor housing and high unemployment.

Particular considerations for primary settings include:

- being clear about the specific roles of different professionals in promoting children's welfare;
- having effective recruitment procedures, including checking that staff are safe to work with children;
- having procedures for dealing with allegations of abuse made against members of staff;
- providing appropriate training for all staff and especially those with special responsibility for child protection;
- identifying child welfare concerns and taking action to address them in partnership with other agencies such as the police child abuse investigation units (CAIU) or NSPCC;
- convening a child protection conference when appropriate.

In practice, joint working is difficult; just getting together three or four professionals from different agencies can prove a huge task – everyone is busy and individuals may be hard to reach. Where funding is separate, agencies will also have different priorities. These are not reasons to avoid joint working, but they are reasons to make sure that proper arrangements are in place and that everyone involved in a meeting or review comes away feeling that it was worthwhile and that they made a useful contribution. Make sure that accurate minutes are taken and agreed by everyone at the end of a meeting; this avoids disagreement later on, over who agreed to do what – especially where funding is concerned (cynics might call this 'covering your back'!).

Making arrangements for this type of working is very time consuming indeed, and in a large school the SENco will almost certainly need someone to help by providing efficient administrative support.

This person may help the SENco or another SMT member to:

1   Set up a comprehensive database of individuals from outside agencies, with a description of their role:

  ■   details of when they work, which days, which hours;
  ■   office base for working (may be more than one);
  ■   contact details – telephone (switchboard/reception, direct line, mobile, email).

    Keeping this information up to date can be a significant job in itself. One way of doing this is to print out the information for each person and get them to confirm or change details on a regular basis when they come in to school. Give individuals as much notice as possible when arranging meetings or assessment/therapy sessions for children. Confirm the arrangements in writing or by email.

2   Book/prepare an appropriate room and inform individuals where this is, including staff on reception. For meetings, make the room as inviting and comfortable as possible. Having a table to sit at can be more businesslike and better for making notes. If a parent is involved, it can be less intimidating to sit in a circle of easy chairs. Arrange for refreshments. If there is a shortage of space in

school, consider asking a neighbouring school or college for the loan of a room.

3   For therapy/assessment sessions secure a room that is free of distraction, comfortable and preferably familiar to the child. You may want to consider having another adult in the vicinity (to guard against any accusations being made by the child about the professional). Expecting a speech and language therapist or educational psychologist to work with a child in a corridor or a corner of a noisy classroom is like saying 'We don't really value what you're doing . . .'. Don't be surprised if it's difficult to get them to come again!

4   Send out any relevant information prior to the meeting so that people can come prepared – including an agenda and any specific requests: 'Kate- please come prepared to give us an update on Harry's progress and your opinion about his ability to transfer successfully to the high school in September.'

5   Spend a little time preparing for the meeting – make sure you know what you hope to achieve. Try to avoid coming out of the meeting with a load of extra work – think beforehand about what can be shared between participants, and how much can be done during the meeting itself – for example, can an administration assistant take minutes (on a laptop)? Be sure to document what different people have agreed to do – and by when. This is particularly important when senior decision makers are involved and have to commit to funding a child's provision. If that person moves on, is ill or on holiday, and there is nothing 'official' recorded, the whole business of getting things sorted out can be delayed because of the funding issue.

6   During the meeting, make sure that everyone speaks and makes a contribution (check beforehand whether it's appropriate for someone to send in a written report rather than have to attend the meeting). Guard against one person 'hogging the floor'. Be assertive in keeping to the agenda and keeping to time.

7   At the end of the meeting, recap main points and decisions taken. Agree a date and time for the next meeting if necessary. Finish on time – this shows that you value people's attendance and will improve your chances of getting them back next time.

Meeting with parents

Meetings in school can be anxiety-inducing for many parents. They can feel intimidated by the school building, the officiousness of administration staff, the 'superiority' of teaching staff and senior managers. And yet, they have a right to be involved in decisions affecting their children and can make a valuable contribution to the discussion about what is needed and what, in fact, works for the child. They may have a totally different perspective on what the 'problems' are and may well have worked out strategies to use in the home that can be usefully adapted to work at school.

There are several ways of overcoming their anxieties:

■ Liaise with your local parent partnership about what support they can give to parents. Many have access to video recordings of review meetings, demonstrating how parents can contribute.

■ Arrange to make a home visit – meeting parents on their own territory can make a big difference and there will then be a 'friendly face' to give them moral support in the meeting (this may be the SENco or another member of staff, a learning support assistant/teaching assistant or another parent). Take an interpreter along if this will help to put parents at ease.

■ Invite parents into school for an informal pre-meeting when you can show them where the meeting will take place, explain what will happen at the meeting and who will be there, and guide parents about the contribution they might make. 'It will be really valuable to have you there, Mrs Lal. You can tell us how Kim has been behaving at home and if she has said anything to you about school.'

■ Encourage parents to make a few notes to bring with them – speaking to a group of professionals can be daunting so having some prompts can be helpful.

■ Communications

Effective communication systems are an important part of inclusion policy and the giving and requesting of information, on all levels, needs to be carefully managed. It's often said that we live in a 'data rich, information poor' society and schools can certainly be in this sort of situation. If baseline data, test scores, teacher assessments and pupils' self-evaluations are not used in a way that impacts directly on what happens in the classsroom, a school will remain information poor. If information about children's home circumstances, learning difficulties or medical needs, is not conveyed to, and understood by, the people teaching them, then some pupils will fail.

Many schools now have intranet systems where a wealth of information can be stored and accessed by staff, perhaps with more sensitive material being password protected and managed by the SENco. The issue in this case can be teachers making the time to read this on a regular basis, and updating it appropriately. I have visited too many schools where the SENco is in possession of a wealth of information on a child with special educational needs, but their class teacher is aware of only a fraction: 'Oh yes, I know he had an assessment for dyslexia but I'm not quite sure how he got on.' 'There are some difficult circumstances in her family but I don't know very much.'

Staff-to-staff

■ Keep concise, relevant information on individual pupils in an easy-to-read format and regularly update it (termly?). Many schools use their intranet for this purpose.

■ Foster a culture of information sharing between staff (this will be helped by making the staffroom a place where people can sit comfortably and chat).

■ Establish daily staff briefings, to include information on individual pupils ('Darren Hart's adoption is going through the courts on Thursday, so he may be anxious and need a bit of extra support').

■ Keep staff noticeboard tidy and up to date.

■ The SENco/INCO could circulate a weekly newsletter to all staff.

■ Create opportunities to learn from each other (lesson observations and feedback; every teacher to take a turn at delivering a ten-minute presentation each term during INSET day or weekly staff meeting – 'These are the steps I've taken to help Jade, who is autistic – can anyone suggest anything else I should be doing?').

■ Hold a 'show and tell' – new resources/equipment/software, an excellent piece of work completed by a pupil, a game devised by an LSA that has worked particularly well with a group of pupils, for instance.

Staff-to-parents/carers-to-staff

If parents have a complaint about schools, it is often about the quality and regularity of information sharing. Schools that manage to keep lines of communication open between staff and parents are going a long way toward building mutually supportive relationships. There are many ways of doing this:

■ Hold termly meetings to report on children's progress. Use meaningful language; 'Level 2' means very little to many parents. Explain what Sarah can do, how she responds to things, what she should work on, what her targets are, how parents can help. Remember to make it a two-way exchange of information – does Sarah seem happy to come to school/read to you at home/be in the Red group? Refer to P levels where appropriate.

■ Give careful consideration to parents' availability – offer different times to accommodate those who work, etc. Have interpreters on hand where appropriate.

■ Introduce home–school diaries. Make sure parents understand how these work, what sort of things they can say – show them an example. For parents with literacy and/or English as an additional language difficulties, consider using symbols: ☺ = Sam had a good day today; ☹ = Sam had a bad day, etc.

■ Send notes home to encourage parents to support their children (Carrie has behaved very well today and was really helpful when the guinea pigs escaped!).

■ Telephone anxious parents to keep them informed.

■ Ensure teachers and senior managers are accessible.

■ Carry out home visits.

Staff-to-pupils-to-staff

It may sound obvious that teachers should have a dialogue with pupils, but the issue is the quality of that dialogue. Is there space in a busy school day to really listen to a child? To 'read between the lines' of what the child is saying?

For many troubled children (for example, those caught up in domestic abuse), their teacher is the one person who could help. Talking about learning objectives and achievements is important, but teachers need to be alert also, to other aspects of a child's life.

Consider how your staff engage with pupils in different sorts of dialogue:

■ Do teachers speak to each individual in their class every day (it's easy to overlook the quiet ones)?

■ Are there opportunities outside the classroom for getting to know each other (field trips, residentials, social events)?

■ Can written notes be used to relay children's thoughts, concerns, fears (pupil journals, graffiti walls, suggestion boxes)?

■ Are pupil surveys used to inform whole school/class practice?

■ Are class/school councils effective?

■ Is circle time used to good effect?

Pupils-to-pupils

Teaching children how to be good listeners is an important part of the emotional literacy curriculum, and a valuable skill for life. For some younger children, just learning to take turns and wait for the speaker to finish is a hard lesson. Circle time is used to great effect here – often with a toy being passed round and children understanding that they can only speak when they are holding it (an exercise that would be useful for many adults!). Schools that are serious about being inclusive and helping children to be tolerant and understanding of diversity will also be taking positive steps to train pupils in communication skills. This might include:

■ peer mentoring and peer tutoring: provide some training in these skills – how to listen, encourage, explain. Use role-play, video and modelling;

■ marking partnerships (the Assessment for Learning material has good ideas on this – see the box below for an example);

■ class/school council;

■ circle time: help children to develop good interpersonal and communication skills, empathy and emotional literacy;

■ circle of friends (see Chapter 4).

See the *Lucky Duck Publishing* catalogue for a wealth of material on these topics: www.luckyduck.co.uk.

Our agreement on marking partnerships (St Elizabeth CE School)

We decided that there were some rules we all needed to keep. When we become marking partners, we all agree to:

■ respect our partner's work because they have done their best and so their work should be valued;

■ try to see how they have tackled their learning objective and only try to improve things that are to do with the learning objective;

■ tell our partner the good things we see in their work;

■ listen to our partner's advice because we are trying to help each other do better in our work;

- look for a way to hep our partner to achieve the learning objective better by giving them a 'closing the gap' improvement to do;

- try to make suggestions as clear as possible;

- get our partner to talk about what they tried to achieve in their work;

- be fair to our partner. We will not talk about their work behind their backs because we wouldn't like them to do it to us and it wouldn't be fair.

Created by children in year 6 at St Elizabeth CE School, Tower Hamlets.

Chapter 4

How can we meet all children's needs?

In this chapter we will consider:

- school experience from the child's perspective;
- learning how 'to be';
- recognising and recording achievement;
- giving children and parents a voice.

Can you remember your time in primary school? What aspects have remained vivid in your memory? This can be a useful question for staff to think about to start a discussion of children's perceptions of school and what they get out of the experience. There's a good chance that they will have retained any negative incidents, along with the more 'novel' experiences.

I remember everyone in my class being 'slippered' (but not why!) and the overpowering feeling of the injustice of it all; making a snow scene out of blocks of salt, playground games, being in the school play, idolising Miss Whitehouse (who wore her cardigans with the buttons at the back – chic!), assemblies, singing, trying to understand (and failing) what I was supposed to be doing in 'Music and Movement' and feeling very anxious. In year 6, I was in charge of going on the bus to the pet shop in town, with three other classmates, and buying a hamster – such responsibility!

I also have a vague memory of a little girl called Eileen who tried hard to be included but was often spurned. She probably had eczema – her skin was very rough and scaly – but at the time none of us understood anything about her condition. We just knew that it felt peculiar to hold her hand and so tried hard not to have to be her partner in games that needed 'pairs'. She often stood alone in the playground. I can't help but think that if we had been told about Eileen's skin condition (and reassured that it wasn't 'catching'), we would all have been much kinder.

■ Learning 'how to be'

Most adults remember very little of the day-to-day lessons where, presumably, most of the curriculum stuff was learnt. It's the trips, the performances, the extra-curricular activities that made most impact. In some schools, these sorts of opportunities have been eroded by the constrictions of a jam-packed curriculum, but it doesn't have to be that way. For children who are 'vulnerable' it is the 'out of school' and 'extended day' activities that offer the richest opportunities for developing as learners and as social beings. Learning how 'to be' with other people, especially other people who are in some way different, is possibly the most important aspect of education.

Pupil swap

The head teacher of a small, all-white school in Cornwall worked with a colleague from a multicultural school in inner-city Bristol to organise a week's 'pupil swap'. Children from a variety of ethnic backgrounds (and four children who had been in war-torn Somalia only weeks before) took part in classroom activities alongside their Cornish peers. They were able to picnic on the beach, learn how to paddle a canoe, visit the Eden project and learn about life in a rural area.

The local community took these children to their hearts, organising a barbeque, beach games and homemade cakes afterwards. The deputy head teacher from the Bristol school had worked very hard not only to secure funding and make all the arrangement, but also to convince parents of the value of the trip.

'We had to work hard to persuade some parents to let us take their children to what seemed to them a foreign land. They associated sleeping in tents with refugee camps and were concerned about the observance of religious and cultural practices. But with the help of our Somali speaking language development worker and other supportive Muslim staff, we were able to reassure them.

The adults who came along had a fantastic time (as well as the children) and were excellent advocates for this type of experience. They were able to convince parents that people in all-white areas can be welcoming and accepting – and encouraged them to spread their wings a little; so many of our families never venture beyond their own small neighbourhoods. I know that it will all be a lot easier next time around.'

Spending so much time with these children gave teachers a real insight into their individual needs.

'One boy in particular came to my attention during the week. At school, he is very well managed and his emotional, social and behavioural difficulties do not pose too much of a problem. But with more freedom and very different boundaries, he needed a lot of one-to-one support.

I learned more about him and what works for him, than I would have in a year's worth of school assessments. The great thing was that he was included in everything, and achieved a lot of success – especially in the rowing, which turned out to be a real strength. We may have never discovered this of course, had we not given him the appropriate opportunity.'

For their part, the pupils from Cornwall met children with a wide range of linguistic and cultural backgrounds. They experienced living and working with children and adults who didn't sound like them, look like them or follow the same cultural practices, but found that they still had a lot in common. This type of first-hand experience was invaluable in preparing them for life in a culturally diverse world.

Learning 'how to be' is, of course, closely allied to 'behaviour' in the traditional sense of conforming to rules, being polite and cooperative and having a good range of social skills. For many children this is an area of significant difficulty. The Code of Practice for SEN identifies an area of special education needs under the heading of 'behaviour, emotional and social development needs'. This group includes children and young people 'who demonstrate features of emotional and behavioural difficulties, who are withdrawn and isolated, disruptive and disturbing, hyperactive and lack concentration; those with immature social skills; and those presenting challenging behaviours arising from other complex needs'.

Teachers are often less enthusiastic about the inclusion of this group than they are about children with other types of difficulties. They often lack confidence in dealing with pupils who are uncooperative in any way and feel powerless to influence their behaviour. There is also concern about the detrimental effect on the learning of other pupils in the class. But a lot can be achieved by a robust whole school behaviour policy and teachers employing basic classroom management techniques consistently.

Pupils with more significant behaviour, emotional and social development needs may require counselling and specific help such as:

- flexible teaching arrangements;

- explicit teaching of social competence and emotional literacy;

- help in developing positive relationships with peers and adults;

- specialised behavioural and cognitive approaches;

- re-challenging or re-focusing to diminish repetitive or self-injurious behaviour.

In addition, Harris (1995) identified strategies most likely to be effective with children who displayed challenging behaviour:

- forming a positive relationship with one particular adult;

- amending the rewards and sanctions system;

- matching learning tasks to known strengths of the pupil;

- focusing on teaching language and communication skills;

- helping the child to anticipate sequences of events and activities;

- allowing the child to opt out of specific activities;

- conveying adult expectations clearly and providing instant feedback;

- providing a written protocol for all staff describing how to respond to specific behaviours.

The causes of unacceptable behaviour stem from personal and environmental factors – the interaction between children and the context in which difficulties occur. Sensory impairment or learning difficulties, for example, can produce feelings of frustration and anger in a child, especially if the learning environment is unsympathetic to their needs. Anxiety about not understanding instructions or finding work too difficult can cause temper tantrums and other forms of challenging behaviour.

Helping pupils to employ some coping strategies can do a lot to reduce angry outbursts (Stop – Think – Do). Teachers need to be able to recognise the warning signs of anxiety in a child and know how to avoid 'pushing their button'.

Increasingly, emotional literacy has been recognised as a key factor in how children behave. Emotional literacy is the ability to manage yourself and your emotions and to understand what other people are thinking and feeling. This has a critical impact on learning and social interaction.

A child or young person who cannot recognise, name and communicate their feelings or thoughts, or who does not understand what others are trying to communicate to them, will become anxious, confused and frustrated and this can lead to unacceptable behaviour. It may be necessary to teach these skills explicitly to some children, rather than assume that they will 'pick them up' eventually. Consider timetabling work with expression cards, puppets and social stories for vulnerable children.

All teachers know that a child's self-esteem is crucial to how they behave and respond to different situations, but it can be difficult sometimes to see past the stroppiness and bravado and remember that the majority of pupils with behaviour, emotional and social development needs are not happy children. They may have been rejected, hurt or neglected by parents. They may have lost loved ones or be suffering from medical problems. They are troubled children whose emotional state leads them into negative behaviour. They may seek attention, even the negative kind, or 'lash out' at a world where they feel everyone is against them.

All of this results in a serious lack of positive feedback and a downward spiralling of self-esteem. The child becomes their own worst enemy and teachers have to look very hard indeed to find something positive to praise. It's important to remember that behaviour, emotional and social development needs may also be associated with exceptionally high levels of ability: when work is insufficiently challenging, boredom can set in and result in the pupil creating their own 'entertainment'.

It is important that teachers get to know pupils well and are able to identify underlying factors that impact on their behaviour, including difficult home circumstances, poor language skills, learning difficulties, attention deficit, misunderstanding of social situations and lack of self-esteem. The key to effective provision for these pupils is establishing a good relationship with them. No book can tell teachers exactly how to do that – there are too many computations. But good two-way communication (see page 50), firm-but-fair discipline and a real interest in learning and teaching combines to build a good base on which to build (see page 69 for what children like in a teacher).

From a leadership position, you need to ensure that curriculum delivery goes hand in hand with effective behavioural, emotional and social development. Check that:

- staff are trained in effective behaviour management;

- you have consistent and agreed behaviour policies, and everyone is familiar with them;

- personal development is valued as highly as academic education;

- there are good partnerships with parents and the wider community;

- all staff have (appropriately) high expectations;

■   staff plan together, and with professionals from other agencies, to meet children's individual needs (informed by accurate assessment).

Circle time and circle of friends

Circle time is regularly used to provide a secure environment where issues can be raised. Participants work within agreed ground rules, listening to each other with patience and without comment or judgement. This contributes to the development of better relationships and positive behaviour, both of which have an important impact on learning and the smooth and harmonious running of a school. The sessions may be linked to the personal, social and health education (PSHE) curriculum, and often consist of weekly meetings lasting half an hour where children sit round in a circle to engage in speaking and listening, games and other activities.

The circle of friends approach can be very effective with pupils whose behaviour has isolated them from other children. They may feel that nobody likes them or wants to be their friend so they have nothing to lose by giving vent to their frustrations and 'kicking off'. The subsequent behaviour of classmates simply confirms their worst fears about themselves and how others see them, and a vicious circle is created.

The 'circle of friends' is a systemic approach that recognises the power of the peer group to be a positive as well as a constraining influence on individual behaviour. It aims to help a child by:

■   creating a support network;

■   reducing instances of challenging behaviour;

■   enabling them to deal successfully with victimisation;

■   increasing their understanding of their own behaviour and different choices they can opt for;

■   providing opportunities for them to make more friends.

The key to success in this approach is a teacher or teaching assistant who is committed to using it and who will be able to give sufficient time to supporting the circle of friends. The child's parent or carer will need to have the approach explained to them and give both their assent and support. New issues may emerge for parents, when for instance children come knocking on the door requesting that their child comes out to play or join in an activity.

The child themself needs to have the approach properly explained in basic terms and needs to accept what is about to occur. Emotions can range from angry resistance through ambivalence to over-the-top enthusiasm, so it will require sound judgment on the teacher's behalf to decide on the way forward.

Setting up a circle of friends

■ Select between six and eight pupils to make up the circle. The teacher's knowledge of children's personalities and strengths will influence the choice – as will each child's enthusiasm for the project.

■ Agree ground rules and explain confidentiality.

■ Agree aims of group – for example to help Darren make and keep friends and to help him get back on track with his behaviour.

■ Elicit from the group some positives about Darren and areas he needs to work on.

■ Brainstorm strategies – for example, 'What can we do when he "kicks off"?' (try to: understand why . . . calm him down . . . distract him . . . count to twenty with him . . . say 'Come and sit here').

■ Agree which strategies can be tried and ensure commitment to these from the group. Be clear with the group about responsibilities, disclosures and boundaries. Let them know what is expected of them and the limits to this.

■ Choose a name for the group (avoiding the child's name).

■ Encourage mutual support in the group and agree on a time and place for weekly meetings to discuss progress and any issues. A main purpose of the meeting is to generate tactics and supportive ideas.

The circle quickly becomes a learning experience for all the children in the group as they talk about feelings, problem solve, listen, empathise, challenge, and work out better ideas for dealing with adults:

> *'We use a tapping code . . . if Darren starts talking when we're on the carpet one of us taps three times on his back or on the floor near him . . . then he shuts up.'*

> *'Darren came into class shouting and dancing after PE and Mrs Bakewell was cross. I said, "He's just feeling a bit excited Miss, he scored a goal."'*

> *'I know a bit more about how Darren feels now because I talk to him more.'*

> *'I feel angry when he gets picked on because I know it upsets him and makes him kick off.'*

By being part of a group dedicated to supporting one of its members, each individual is given the implicit message that it is safe to have needs, to find coping in some situations difficult and that, when you do, you can rely on others for support. This is important because it is unlikely to be the focus child alone who has feelings that are difficult to manage or behaviours that others find antagonising.

> *Teacher: 'How can we help him when he loses his temper?'*

> *Jane: 'Talk to him . . . help him calm down . . . stay with him . . . comfort him . . . distract him.'*

> *It's likely that this was as much about what Jane needed and wanted when she lost her temper, as what was appropriate for the focus child.*

Working with peers

Many schools encourage children to work with peers in their own or other classes for mutual learning, support and mediation. This can happen in many ways, for example:

■ Peer support – pupils directly support peers or younger pupils, perhaps helping with reading, or simply listening to them, to help build self-esteem and develop positive behaviour patterns. This can result in a supportive one-to-one relationship between two pupils and often helps the 'supporter' as well as the 'supported'. Providing training for this kind of work can make it very effective.

■ Peer mediation – when young people are trained to mediate disagreements between peers, such as name-calling, bullying, fighting and quarrelling. The approach is usually one of group support which enables children and young people to understand the hurt that they have caused so that each person comes away from the mediation with a positive experience and the sense that the outcome is fair to both sides.

Mediation is one of a number of approaches that have proved to be helpful in addressing bullying. 'Mediation is a structured process in which a neutral third party assists voluntary participants to resolve their dispute' (Stacey and Robinson 1997).

■ Recognising and recording achievement

National Curriculum teacher assessments, test scores and league tables tell only part of the achievements story. Inclusive schools are good at looking beyond these indicators and adopting a more holistic view of the child.

How is achievement identified and celebrated in your school – especially for children who are not teacher-pleasers, not academic, not particularly good at music or sport?

Ask staff to make a list of all the opportunities for children to 'shine' and be praised outside the usual parameters of 'academic' achievement, and add their ideas to the ones opposite.

What did you do today to make yourself proud?

Got to school on time.

Remembered my books/sports kit/home/school diary.

Answered a question correctly.

Helped a friend.

Spoke to someone who was alone in the playground.

Shared my crisps.

Lent my ruler/calculator to someone.

Had a good idea.

Cleaned out the guinea pigs.

Watered the plants.

Tidied the art cupboard.

Collected in the books.

Made a display.

Stopped a fight.

Played a game without cheating.

Worked with a partner.

Finished a piece of work.

Sent a card to someone who is poorly.

Said thank you.

Asked a good question.

Said something nice about someone.

Helped with fundraising.

Organised a discussion/meeting/work party.

Owned up when I did something wrong.

Said 'sorry'.

(See Hannell 2004 for further ideas)

Part of being able to recognise and praise positive behaviour is having an awareness of the vast range of different human strengths and abilities. The challenge is to seek out, celebrate and build on each child's way of looking at the world.

■ **Social and humanitarian ability** – getting along with other people. Caring about how others feel and think; having compassion and a sense of justice; seeing others' point of view.

■ **Emotional ability** – understanding and identifying our own feelings and other people's: responding to others in a sympathetic way.

■ **Spiritual ability** – an ability to appreciate elements of life that are outside our understanding; being able to experience 'awe and wonder'.

■ **Linguistic ability** – understanding and using words/symbols, spoken and written, to reason, explain, question, persuade and entertain.

■ **Mathematical ability** – understanding concrete and abstract relationships in the use of numbers, codes, symbols, diagrams, shape and space.

■ **Scientific ability** – understanding and explaining the natural and scientific world through the use of observation, identification, classification, investigation and analysis.

■ **Mechanical/technical ability** – understanding, designing and manipulating tools, materials, equipment and machinery.

■ **Visual/spatial abilities** – seeing things in the physical world accurately and in detail, but also able to manipulate images 'in the mind's eye'.

■ **Auditory/sonal ability** – the ability to hear, produce and manipulate sounds with attention to pitch, tone and expression. Musicians obviously have this, but so do poets, writers and public speakers, as demonstrated in their use of rhythm, pattern and alliteration.

■ **Movement/somatic ability** – ability associated with body movement and use of all the different senses.

See Wallace *et al.* (2004: 147) for a teacher's checklist of different abilities and a menu of activities to promote them (159).

Some of these abilities will be more in evidence outside the classroom. Schools are becoming ever more adventurous in their curricula. Exhorted by officialdom to break free of 'the strategy' and place more of an emphasis on creativity, enjoyment and enterprise, teachers are working hard to shape what they teach to meet the needs of their pupils and the local community. This is resulting, in many cases, in a much wider range of learning experiences that provide more children with opportunities to succeed.

But schools need to be aware of the bigger picture of a child's life and the interests they pursue outside school hours. Is it karate club, piano lessons or dog walking for the local kennel club? For many children, their passion will lie outside the school gates and remain an untapped resource. How many of your pupils, for example, have private piano lessons and reach a level of competency that equips them to play a piece of music for assembly? Are they given this opportunity? Does the school recognise and value skills and abilities developed outside school in a more meaningful way than presenting them with bits of paper in assembly every Friday?

Some pupils have significant responsibilities in the home; they are adept at feeding and changing babies, keeping toddlers amused, shopping for food, preparing meals and keeping the house clean and tidy. They are developing many (transferable) skills, but seldom receive any recognition for this from their teachers.

Starring: you

One teacher begins afternoon sessions with a brief artistic performance: children play musical instruments, sing, recite a poem or perform a play or dance. These performances create a very positive and relaxed atmosphere and set the tone for the rest of the afternoon. They also provide opportunities for children to showcase their talents and help to develop their confidence in performing to an audience; self-esteem blossoms.

Other ideas include a 'star pupil' board in the classroom, with a photo and details of a child's accomplishments, and pupil-to-pupil interviews in front of the class, where a child is given 'celebrity treatment'.

Individual education plans

Children who have significant difficulties in school relating to learning, socialisation and/or behaviour may be helped by the implementation of an individual education/behaviour plan (IEP). The IEP is usually devised to run for a short period of time and has three or four short-term targets that are,

- **s**pecific;
- **m**easurable;
- **a**ttainable;
- **r**elevant;
- **t**ime-limited.

Ideally, the IEP should be set up with teachers and parents involved as equal partners. The pupil should also be able to give their views and have these included in the planning. The class teacher should always have input into an IEP, even if the SENco acts as adviser in its design and implementation.

The plan should involve structured approaches with an emphasis on success and may involve one-to-one or small group teaching on a regular basis. How the teaching is to be resourced is an important issue. There are several questions to be answered:

- **What** is to be used? What materials or learning packages are needed?

- **Who** is going to carry out the intervention? If a teaching assistant or learning support assistant is going to be involved, there should be teacher supervision for planning and monitoring.

- **When** is the work going to be done and for how long? When will it be reviewed?

- **Where** will the sessions take place? A corner of a noisy, distraction-filled classroom will not usually be the best place.

IEPs provide a means of prioritising goals for children – especially when they have several areas of difficulty. They also enable monitoring of the smallest achievements, which provides positive feedback for both pupil and parents. Most teachers are familiar now with the P scales but may still be in the early stages of using them to best effect in the classroom. These descriptors of pre-National Curriculum level achievement are invaluable for recording the very small steps of progress made by some pupils with special educational needs, and in planning appropriately for them.

Capturing information about a child's diverse achievements can be challenging. Needless to say, a mark book does not do it! You need to think about a portfolio of samples of work, records of achievements, certificates, commendations, badges, etc. backed up by digital photographs, with an explanation written on the back. 'This is Jack standing by the timeline he made with help from Lucy and Mrs Roberts. Jack showed Mr Adams the dates of Queen Victoria's birth and death and worked out how old she was. He could describe three ways that life had changed for children during that period.'

Of course, this amounts to quite an issue in terms of storage over time, so there must be a way of collating it all onto a couple of sides of A4 paper at the end of each year. Provide each child with a box to take their work home and keep it safe (ask local businesses to donate boxes for this purpose – shoe boxes, box files, clean packing cartons used in manufacturing, etc.).

■ Giving children and parents a voice

The NSPCC used a powerful slogan some time ago: 'He needs a good listening to.' It referred to the traditional school culture of teachers talking at pupils and not paying enough attention to getting them to talk to us. It implied that for many children whose home circumstances are less than satisfactory, having someone to talk to is very important indeed. In fact, being able to talk with a trusted adult is valuable for every child, and often that person will be a teacher or a teaching assistant. The use of peer mediators and 'listening partners' is also growing and can provide valuable support when pupils are appropriately prepared for this role.

Giving children and parents a voice is perhaps the single most effective way of developing as an inclusive school. But this is often easier said than done. It is one thing to get the views of confident, articulate people, but quite another to get feedback from those who are reticent – for whatever reason. A simple checklist can be useful for this (see the box below).

Here's what I think

Pupil feedback	never	sometimes	usually	always
I like being at this school				
I find out new things in lessons				
Lessons are interesting and fun				
I get help when I get stuck with my work				
I have to work hard				
Teachers show me how to make my work better				
Other children in my class behave well				
Other children in my class are friendly towards me				
There is an adult I can go to if I am worried at school				
Teachers treat me fairly				
Teachers listen to my ideas				
I am trusted to do things on my own				

(Adapted from Cheminais 2004)

What helps you to learn at school?

The information below was collected as part of a project on Dyslexia Friendly Schools and reported in Peer (2005). Pupils were encouraged to fill in questionnaires with the help of their parents but to respond in their own words, about their own experiences. The responses serve to focus teachers' attention on what might really work with their children, and all schools could learn a great deal about whether or not they are meeting the needs of their children by running a similar activity. Pupils said:

- At the start of a lesson a teacher should make it clear exactly what they want us to do.

- Show us, don't just tell us.

- Give us time to listen.

- It is easier if the teacher is enthusiastic.

- The use of pictures and materials make it easier to understand.

- We like to be able to ask questions and to have teachers check that we are doing the right thing.

- Good teachers give help if you get stuck and are patient if you need things repeated.

- Teachers should be nice, and should not shout if you get things wrong. They should be patient with your mistakes.

Canvassing parents and carers can also provide a wealth of information about how well a school is doing and highlight strengths and weaknesses which staff need to be aware of. There are different ways of doing this, but questionnaires and interviews/meetings are the main ones. Both need to be planned and well thought out if they are to be really worthwhile.

Schools often complain that some parents don't turn up for parents' evenings – often those who teachers would really like to see because their children are the ones who most need support and encouragement from home. We have to remind ourselves that some parents are intimidated by 'authority figures' like teachers; they have memories of bad experiences in their own schooling; they fear criticism of the way they are bringing up their children. A lot of good public relations work is needed if they are ever to feel comfortable about coming into school, including possibly visiting parents on their own territory at home. Consider, too, the opportunities offered to parents to be involved in the school if they don't speak very good English, or use a wheelchair, or work long hours. How do you support adult learning and empower parents to help their own children?

Effective parent/carer participation – a checklist

Consider	For example
In any type of consultation, we should be clear about objectives and boundaries. How can we convince them that the topic is relevant to them and their children, and that their opinion counts?	New recreational facilities; fundraising; school meals policy; curriculum provision; teaching and learning; target-setting; behaviour policy; uniforms; staffing.
Which parents and carers will be involved? The 'usual suspects' – interested, supportive parents, or can we go the extra mile and persuade some of the 'hard to reach' to get involved?	Consider carefully how to ensure those with additional needs can be involved on an equal basis. This may involve looking at physical access, interpreters, audio/visual support, transport (can you lay on a bus to collect people?). Timing is important – during the day they may be at work, in the evening they can't leave the children. Consider running a meeting twice and asking parents which they can attend. Can you provide a crèche? Printed material must be concise, easy to read and provided in community languages.
At what stage shall we consult? This will affect the level of people's commitment to the process and the amount of satisfaction they get out of it.	Involve them as early as possible once you have a firm idea/proposal backed up by appropriate information and the necessary research. Don't waste their time.
How much power do they have?	Identify the powers being shared/delegated. Make it clear how each stage of the decision making process relates to the next.
Have you considered equal opportunities issues?	Are you talking to parents/carers of children with special educational needs and those from different ethnic backgrounds?
Which methods are most appropriate? Consider how to involve hard-to-reach groups.	Meetings – in school, local community facilities, the pub, church, someone's home; web-based intranet surveys; letters and questionnaires; telephone calls; voting; workshops; individual consultations.
What about feedback?	Parents and carers want to know how their views have been taken into account, and if not, why not. So identify what has changed as a direct result of the process and inform them. This needs to be presented in easy-to-understand formats and possibly in different languages.

School councils

Many schools have a school council that gives pupils a real voice in how their school is run and can be very effective in achieving inclusive practice. The most effective councils are not too big and have:

- regular meetings, with the link teacher always attending;
- feedback from class councils that meet regularly;
- good communication between representatives and their class;
- training for school council members;
- smaller groups (subcommittees) working on specific events or issues;
- a bank account or budget (however small);
- annual evaluations.

A school council can:

- enable children to be active stakeholders in their school;
- provide an extra network of communication throughout the school;
- teach the basics about our political systems;
- assist with the organisation of special events and fundraising activities;
- add an important dimension to the review of behaviour management and associated policy and practice;
- improve standards of behaviour;
- build pupils' confidence and self-esteem;
- encourage shy and disaffected pupils to be more involved;
- reduce the likelihood of bullying;
- offer pupils the opportunity to learn additional valuable skills;
- decrease teacher time spent on petty misbehaviour.

Successful school councils have been seen to: campaign to the local council and get their toilets sorted out; re-design the school cafeteria and lunch menu; reduce bullying by introducing a telephone helpline for victims; design and sell new homework diaries; change the school uniform.

For more information on setting up and running a school council see the Liverpool City Council website or the Schools Council website (see www.liverpool.gov.uk/community_and_living/young_people/schools-councils/index.asp and www.schoolcouncils.org).

Chapter 5

How can we over
barriers to learn

In this chapter we will consider how to overcome barriers to learning by thinking about:

■ creating an inclusive learning environment;

■ behaviour management;

■ teaching and learning.

■ Creating an inclusive learning environment

This is about more than the physical environment, of course, though furniture and furnishings, wall displays, storage of equipment, etc. can have an important bearing on how comfortable children are in a classroom and how well they 'perform'.

The creation of a truly inclusive learning environment involves reassuring pupils that:

■ they can take risks;

■ it's OK to make mistakes sometimes;

■ they can ask for help (and receive it);

■ effort is rewarded, as well as achievement;

. types of ability are valued;

different learning styles are acknowledged and catered for.

There is a lot of very useful information available on identifying barriers to learning and then devising ways of eliminating those barriers. You will find some of the most valuable books and websites listed on pages 99–105. Make sure that the staff library has a good selection of this type of material – but short, practical CPD sessions for staff will also be effective in demonstrating different types of difficulties that children experience and ways of overcoming them. These can be led by:

- yourself, your SENco, a teaching assistant or learning support assistant;

- a colleague from a neighbouring school – perhaps a special school;

- a local authority adviser, professional consultant/trainer;

- a parent of a child with a disability.

In parallel, staff should be talking to each other about children they teach – the problems they encounter, and ways of reducing/eliminating them. Being able to observe an effective teacher (in real time or on video) is one of the very best ways of demonstrating, and spreading, good practice. Reflecting on one's own practice and identifying any areas to be addressed can be a useful exercise for staff. The checklist in the box 'What can I do?' may be a useful tool for this.

What can I do?

I remove/reduce barriers to learning by:

Identifying children's individual needs, for example:

Seeking advice from SENco, support agencies, parents, written information, for example:

Adjusting the classroom environment, for example:

Differentiating the curriculum, for example:

Positively managing pupils' behaviour, for example:

Planning and evaluating with support staff, for example:

Discussing progress of pupils with SENco, learning mentors, support staff, for example:

Utilising a range of teaching strategies, for example:

Establishing systems of peer support, for example:

Contributing to pupils' IEPs and linking them to lesson planning, for example:

Using appropriate assessment, for example:

Involving children in decisions made about their learning, for example:

The physical environment

The physical environment plays an important role in every child's learning and enjoyment, so it's essential to look analytically at all areas of the school, not only classrooms but also the playground/sports field, hall/dining room and toilets. If you're lucky enough to have a parents'/community room, this should also be attractive, welcoming, comfortable and accessible.

It can be difficult to be analytical about familiar surroundings, so if in doubt invite an 'outsider' to look around the school and give you feedback. Fairly low-cost improvements can make a big difference and this is a great way to involve parents who are much more confident with a paint brush than they are with helping their child with maths homework. Get someone to do a 'trial run' with a wheelchair to check out accessibility issues (a good project for pupils). Don't underestimate the importance of toilets and cloakrooms. There are special considerations to do with handrails, wheelchair access, etc. which your local support service can advise about, but there are also basic points to consider with regard to all users:

- cleanliness;

- doors that close properly and are easy to lock and unlock;

- toilet paper;

- soap;

- hand towels/driers;

- adequate supervision so that toilets don't become favourite haunts for bullies.

This all sounds very obvious, but there are plenty of children who avoid going to the toilet all day rather than use 'scary' loos.

Encourage teachers to assess the general accessibility of their classrooms:

- Is it welcoming?

- Can all pupils see the board, TV monitor, teacher and displays?

- Can bright light be dimmed or cut out by window blinds?

- Do windows work so that fresh air can be let in?

- Do radiators work so that there is adequate temperature control?

- Is drinking water available?

- Can pupils and adults move around the classroom easily and safely?

■ Are resources clearly labelled and reachable?

■ Is the classroom atmosphere calm?

■ Is good use made of display?

■ Is furniture and equipment the right height/variable height for individual pupils?

■ Is there a quiet, distraction-free area in the classroom?

■ Is use made of visual timetables?

■ Is written information produced in a range of formats/languages?

■ Is there specially adapted equipment for those who need it? Find out about low-cost adaptations to equipment to be used in design and technology, maths and science investigations.

■ Ensure access to appropriate IT equipment for the lesson. Simply changing the settings on the 'accessibility' options, keyboard or mouse menus in the controls panel may be a great help. Explore switch access, roller balls, big keyboards/ keyguards, touch screens, voice recognition.

Disability discrimination

Part IV of the Disability Discrimination Act states that schools must not discriminate against children with disabilities in terms of admissions, exclusions and 'education and associated services,' a term that covers every aspect of the life of the school. A *Code of practice*, published by the Disability Rights Commission, provides guidance on the way that these duties operate, with examples illustrating how they apply in practical situations. Ofsted expects to see evidence of practical adjustments being made in the classroom and in other areas of school life.

If parents think that their child has been discriminated against, they have a right of redress by making a claim of disability discrimination to the special educational needs and disability tribunal. If the tribunal finds that a school has discriminated unlawfully against a disabled pupil it can order any remedy that it sees fit, except financial compensation.

All schools are required to prepare, review and implement accessibility plans outlining how the school will:

- increase pupils' participation in the curriculum;

- improve the physical environment to increase access to all services provided by the school;

- improve the delivery of information to disabled pupils and their families;

- establish good links with support agencies;

- provide training for staff on how to meet the needs of children with disabilities and complex health needs.

The checklist below outlines some of the considerations for a school preparing for a child with disabilities and/or health needs:

- How will the child get to and from school?

- How will the child get around the building, into classrooms, toilets? Do we need to install ramps and handrails or relocate facilities to the ground floor?

- What issues arise for school outings?

- Will quiet distraction-free workspaces and/or dinner times be necessary and available?

- At what level are the child's self-help skills (eating, drinking, toileting)?

- What equipment will be needed (adjustable height/sloping tables, nappy disposal, standing frames, adapted technology)?

- Does the child have medical needs? Who will administer medication?

- What issues arise for the child at play times and lunch, e.g. not coping with noise in the playground/dinner hall?

- How will the child access curriculum levels? Notify curriculum coordinators in relation to planning and providing resources.

■ Does the child need adult support in the classroom, at lunch, at play time, around the school?

■ What additional skills will adults need in relation to learning, social and emotional, physical and medical needs? What is the plan for training staff?

Children with complex health needs should have health care plans specifically detailing:

■ the level of support to be provided;

■ particular procedures that should be carried out, by whom and the training they can expect;

■ protocols for exchanging information between agencies (with clearly defined lines of responsibility and named contacts);

■ additional risk assessments required for that particular child – who is responsible for carrying them out;

■ any special health care needs that may affect the child's use of services such as transport or play activities, implementation of therapy programmes, etc.;

■ the use, storage and maintenance of any equipment;

■ arrangements for the provision of education or associated services when the child is too unwell to attend school or is in hospital;

■ parental wishes for the child;

■ information on the manner in which the child prefers any task to be carried out, in order to ensure consistency of approach across all settings;

■ any anticipated changes in the child's condition or care routine;

■ arrangements for reviewing the plan.

Particular adjustments needed for pupils (or staff) with physical or sensory difficulties may have to be made in consultation with a member of the local authority's support service, who will also be able to advise on special aids and items of equipment. Getting to know pupils and their parents/carers will help you and your staff make the right adjustments. Once adjustments have been made, remember to ask the pupils for feedback and be prepared to act on their advice.

Behaviour management

Good behaviour management is a whole school issue. Whichever particular approach is adopted in school, every teacher's repertoire of skills should include effective management techniques and basic good practice, such as being in a room ready to greet pupils, modelling good manners and using the agreed methods of rewards and sanctions consistently. An understanding of the ABC of behaviour management is essential:

- A – antecedents – situations that trigger unwanted behaviour;

- B – behaviour – what the child does;

- C – consequences – what does the pupil get out of the behaviour (reward or punishment).

This model can provide a useful structure for observing behaviour in the classroom and identifying patterns. It can also form the basis of a behaviour diary. A further dimension also needs to be considered, however, and that is the child's emotional state. For example, a pupil who is confident and 'emotionally literate' will cope better with being criticised than a child who feels that the world is against them.

The underlying approach of the ABC model is to identify and avoid the 'triggers' wherever possible and deal effectively with undesirable behaviour through effective classroom management.

Antecedents

A variety of elements in the situation and/or environment can lead to positive or negative behaviour.

The teacher

Does the teacher:

■ make pupils feel welcome when they arrive every morning?

■ prepare well for lessons and get organised?

■ stay calm and unruffled, have a sense of humour?

■ show enthusiasm for what they are teaching?

■ make sure they are always consistent – 'firm but fair'?

■ understand the individual needs of pupils?

The curriculum

■ Are tasks matched to pupil needs?

■ Is there planned progression and continuity?

■ Is the subject matter relevant to pupils?

The lesson

■ Do children know what they are aiming to learn?

■ Are there clear, achievable goals, building on what has already been learned?

■ Do the pupils know how to get help?

■ Are support staff knowledgeable and deployed flexibly?

■ Is there variety in task, pace, style of delivery?

■ Are there opportunities to use different learning styles?

■ Does every pupil achieve success every day?

Grouping

■ Do teachers consider the dynamics of different groups and provide opportunities for children to work alongside:
  - children of similar ability (this allows pupils to feel comfortable, help each other along);
  - friends (this makes for better enjoyment, which makes for better learning);

- children who are more able (this provides opportunities for learning from peer tutoring, observing how others approach things, how they behave);
- children who are less able (this allows pupils to be in a position of 'teacher' and develops patience and empathy).

Rules

■ Are there clear rules for behaviour displayed in every room?

■ Were the pupils involved in agreeing them?

■ Are they referred to and upheld consistently?

Emotional literacy

■ Is there a whole school ethos promoting emotional literacy through every aspect of the curriculum?

■ Do pupils have the self-control and self-esteem necessary to be successful learners?

■ Do staff understand their own reactions to pupils' behaviour?

Family background and in-child factors
Are teachers aware of:

■ circumstances that may be impacting on an individual, for example if they are young carers?

■ the implications of specific medical, psychological or neurological conditions that need to be addressed?

■ cultural issues that may impact on behaviour and learning?

Behaviours

Negative behaviour may be expressed in a variety of ways and can be either low level (but persistent) or more challenging and episodic. It may include:

■ disrupting the work of others;

■ calling/shouting out;

- answering back;

- leaving their seat;

- wandering around the room;

- throwing, pulling, pushing, poking;

- refusal to work/not listening;

- not doing homework;

- destruction of work;

- verbal abuse;

- physical aggression;

- stubborn non-engagement;

- crying;

- leaving the room;

- in extreme circumstances, a heightened emotional state can lead to an epileptic fit.

Such behaviour may be designed to:

- gain attention;

- demonstrate power;

- avoid work – especially if it is too difficult, too easy or too boring;

- prevent the teacher and/or peers identifying a difficulty/inability.

It is valuable to be able to observe a child during lessons and/or break times and record the sort of behaviour seen – and the consequences. This is very difficult to do whilst teaching – ask teachers to work in pairs and observe children in each other's lessons. Is there a pattern to antecedents/behaviours? Is there a difference in how the child behaves in different lessons?

Consequences

It is important to teach pupils that consequences can be anticipated. This requires all staff to be consistent in applying rewards and sanctions, but means then that children have to be responsible for their own plight. If they choose a certain course of action, they know that a particular consequence will follow.

Positive consequences – praise and rewards for good behaviour – are much more powerful than sanctions for bad behaviour. 'Catching them being good' and praising them for it, will reinforce desirable behaviour, increase children's self-esteem and demonstrate to other children exactly what you are hoping for. Try to ensure that such acknowledgement is given immediately and precisely. Instead of saying 'You have behaved well today', be specific: 'You really listened well today and remembered to put up your hand instead of shouting out. Well done.'

Individual teachers have to accept responsibility for teaching good behaviour, sometimes quite explicitly. Remember that for some children with special educational needs and/or English as an additional language, language-based approaches are not effective – think about using pictures, photographs and role play. 'Behaviour can be an area where we expect so much and teach so little' (Galvin *et al.* 1999).

Work with staff to establish a hierarchy of strategies for dealing with inappropriate behaviour:

- Quell low level disruption by using eye contact or moving nearer to the pupil, saying a pupil's name or writing it on the board.

- Ask if there is anything needed, such as support or a different resource. Careful questioning can deflect the unwanted behaviour and direct the child back 'on task'.

- Issue a warning with a reminder of the appropriate behaviour that is expected. Place the responsibility firmly in the lap of the pupil: for example, 'You can choose to do "a" or "b" but if you choose "b", this is what will happen.' Remind the pupil of the rules, clearly displayed, that have been drawn up and agreed by everybody.

■ Stay calm, but show that you understand how the pupil is feeling and intend to do something about it. 'I can see that you're upset/angry/frustrated and this is affecting your learning . . . I want to help you so this is what I suggest . . .'.

■ Use appropriate sanctions that have been agreed and are understood by pupils, staff and parents and may include:
  – making a note in the home/school diary or on the daily report form;
  – time out from the group/classroom;
  – keeping the pupil in during break/lunch to finish work;
  – staying after school (detention);
  – reporting to year tutor/head teacher/parents;
  – temporary/permanent exclusion.

Avoid:

■ squaring up: face-to-face positions can be confrontational so turn slightly to introduce an angle;

■ invading personal space: aim to keep 25–30 cm between you and the pupil;

■ threatening movements, such as wagging a finger: good gestures are where you show the palms of your hands, or use them to push down – 'Let's calm down';

■ sarcasm: it may not be understood and can exacerbate the situation.

■ backing the child into a corner, both physically and metaphorically: always give them a way out.

Individual Behaviour Plans (IBPs)

These can provide pupils with clear and achievable targets and help to identify and quantify progress: decide on the main priority and use specific objectives like the examples below. Try to change only *one* behaviour at a time. If there are curricular issues as well as behavioural ones, the IEP can include both kinds of target, but you may have to accept that academic progress takes a back seat while behaviour difficulties are prioritised (see McNamara 1999 for practical approaches to contracts, personal goals, etc.).

Managing behaviour

Positive behaviour management strategies include the use of voice and body language, questioning skills, sharing attention between all members of a class, modelling good manners and consideration, and adopting appropriate methods of reward and sanctions.

■ Condemn the action, not the child: 'That was a cruel thing to do', rather than 'You're a very cruel and naughty boy.' Attaching negative labels to children tends to result in a self-fulfilling situation; you give them a reputation to live down to rather than positive expectations to live up to.

■ Catch them being good and use praise to reinforce good behaviour. Moderate the way in which you do this, to suit the age and temperament of the individual (older pupils may not welcome public acclaim, but a word in private – and/or to parents – can be well-received).

■ Don't bear a grudge. Be prepared to wipe the slate clean after an incident and help the pupil to start afresh.

■ Use systems such as 'traffic lights' and noise gauges (teach pupils the use of different voices for discussion groups, pair work, etc. to prevent too much escalation of noise).

■ Ensure that tasks are matched to pupils' abilities.

■ Vary the ways in which pupils are grouped, ensuring that a child with behaviour difficulties has access to good role models.

■ Introduce regular breaks into the lesson – change of pace/activity; introduce movement, 'brain gym' (exercises developed by Paul Dennison and others to stimulate brain activity).

■ Enhance the pupil's self-esteem. Make sure they succeed at something every lesson/day.

■ Make explicit to pupils the effects of their behaviour.

■ Be clear about what constitutes unacceptable behaviour, referring regularly to the classroom code of conduct.

■ Use humour, where appropriate, to deflect anger and avoid confrontation (but avoid humiliating pupils).

■ Instigate a 'help needed' or 'time out' facility such as a card that a child can hold up when they need support or time to 'defuse'.

■ Teach relaxation and anger-management strategies.

■ Where possible, foster and encourage parental support.

■ Identify learning difficulties and provide effective support.

■ Apply controls, restrictions and sanctions fairly and consistently.

■ Award appropriate rewards.

(East and Evans 2006)

■ Teaching and learning

Being aware of different preferred learning styles and individual needs is central to being a good teacher. In good practitioners it is instinctive. It boils down to four main essentials:

■ knowing the child;

■ knowing and being enthusiastic about what you are teaching;

■ being aware of the barriers to learning;

■ developing ways to overcome them.

There is a plethora of information now available about reducing/eliminating barriers to achievement; long lists detail what to try with a child who has a particular difficulty or 'condition'. For practical purposes, teachers can be encouraged to consider how they identify and address barriers to learning under six main headings: access to input, learning objectives, tasks/activities, responses, support and outcomes.

Access to input

Can pupils see, hear, understand the input? Difficulties may not be immediately apparent. Make sure you check; ask them, watch them, question them. If any pupil can't see, hear or understand – what can the teacher do to rectify the situation? Solutions can be straightforward – moving a child nearer to the board, washing their specs, making sure they can see your face when you speak, to more elaborate arrangements like having a teaching assistant or a peer buddy to explain in a different way, or a different language.

Learning objectives

The lesson objectives may be to weigh vegetables and pieces of fruit using standard measures, record the weights accurately and estimate how many would be needed to make up a kilogram; but the first target for some children may be to:

- learn the names of the vegetables and fruit;
- understand 'light' and 'heavy', 'mass' and 'weight';
- use balance scales efficiently;
- understand standard measures.

For others, the main target may be specified in an IEP and be 'to work with a partner' or 'to stay on task for five minutes'. Teachers need to have confidence about making decisions of this sort. When planning for children with significant difficulties in learning, familiarity with the P scales will prove useful.

Tasks/activities

If every child is tasked with doing the same activity in the same way (with the expectation that they will produce similar results) some will fail and others will be bored because they aren't sufficiently challenged. Differentiating – sometimes by making only minor adjustments – is crucial in enabling every child to succeed (see box below). Teachers who understand how learning develops acquire this skill almost intuitively.

In the example given above, some children may be asked to estimate the weights of a wide variety of foods, record their findings in various ways, compare different groups of food, etc. Others may be required to determine which is the heavier of two different vegetables and tell the rest of the class about their findings in the plenary.

Responses

This will be closely linked to the task, but teachers can get hooked up on expecting written work in books and real learning can get sacrificed. Children who, for whatever reason, find it difficult to record their work on paper can sometimes use other means of demonstrating what they know:

- audio recording – a partner or teaching assistant asks them what they have learned;

- video recording – a partner or teaching assistant films the child during the activity and asks them to explain;

- digital photo – with caption written by a teaching assistant;
- verbal feedback to teacher/teaching assistant/group;
- line up the foods in weight order (real foods or paper cut-outs on a display/ in folder).

Support

This is about providing moral support, boosting confidence and keeping a child on task as well as providing extra explanation, jogging the memory and 'plugging the gaps'. It's also about providing appropriate materials and resources and concrete examples where possible (the role of a teaching assistant/learning support assistant is considered below).

Outcomes

This should be more than a completed page in an exercise book, or a tick in a box. It should be a child feeling that they have achieved something and feeling good about themself.

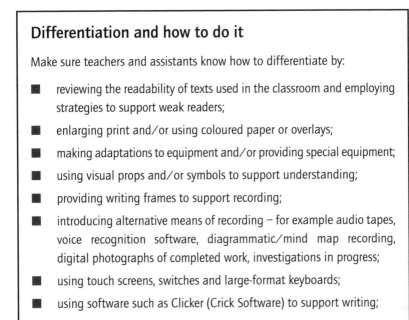

Differentiation and how to do it

Make sure teachers and assistants know how to differentiate by:

- reviewing the readability of texts used in the classroom and employing strategies to support weak readers;
- enlarging print and/or using coloured paper or overlays;
- making adaptations to equipment and/or providing special equipment;
- using visual props and/or symbols to support understanding;
- providing writing frames to support recording;
- introducing alternative means of recording – for example audio tapes, voice recognition software, diagrammatic/mind map recording, digital photographs of completed work, investigations in progress;
- using touch screens, switches and large-format keyboards;
- using software such as Clicker (Crick Software) to support writing;

- adapting tasks or providing alternative activities – breaking down new learning into small chunks;

- using a multi-sensory approach (see box, 'Multi-sensory teaching and learning');

- providing and managing support from adults or peers;

- allowing extra time for completion of tasks and/or providing opportunities for preparation time, perhaps with the help of a teaching assistant remembering that children with special needs often have to make a lot more effort than other children to understand a new concept, complete a task, concentrate on what is being said.

Multi-sensory teaching and learning

Auditory   Discussion, active listening, oral feedback, investigative reporting, interviewing.

Visual   Watching videos/DVD, using websites, making mind maps, brainstorming, highlighting, designing, drawing, visualising.

Kinaesthetic   Building models, touching, manipulating, carrying out investigations and experiments.

Strategies for children with physical and sensory difficulties

For children with physical and sensory difficulties, there are additional strategies to consider – many of them prove useful to all pupils.

For pupils with physical difficulties:

- teach alternative ways of recording work.

- allow pupils to leave lessons a few minutes early to avoid busy corridors and give time to get to next lesson.

- plan to cover work missed through medical or physiotherapy appointments.

■ be sensitive to fatigue, especially at the end of the school day.

■ set homework earlier in the lesson so instructions are not missed.

■ speak directly to the pupil rather than through a teaching assistant.

■ let pupils make their own decisions.

■ arrange a work/subject buddy.

For pupils with a hearing impairment:

■ Find out the nature and degree of the pupil's hearing loss.

■ Check the best seating position (e.g. away from the hum of overhead projectors, computers, etc.) with the child's best-hearing ear toward the speaker.

■ Check that the pupil can see your face for facial expressions and lip reading. Avoid talking when facing the blackboard, or obscuring your face with a book.

■ When talking to the child use your normal voice at normal speed. It does not help to try to emphasise your lip-patterns or to raise your voice.

■ Indicate the topic to be talked about so that the child can anticipate the vocabulary.

■ Avoid talking in a situation where the light is behind you, for example near the window, where you appear in silhouette to the child. Also avoid places where your face is in strong shadow.

■ Talk at a normal rate, not too fast, yet not too slowly.

■ Provide a list of vocabulary, context and visual clues, especially for new subjects.

■ During class discussions allow one pupil to speak at a time and indicate where the speaker is.

■ Check that any aids are working and if there is any other specialist equipment available.

■ Allow the child to turn around to see other children when they are talking.

■ Ensure that the child has understood instructions, remembering that high frequency hearing loss often causes ambiguity.

■ Be aware that difficulty with spelling can result from hearing loss, particularly with word endings, for example walk, walks, walked and walking.

■ Consider learning British Sign Language or sign supported English.

For pupils with a visual impairment:

■ Check that glasses are worn when they should be, and that they are clean!

■ Always provide the pupil with his own copy of the text with enlarged print. Good contrast and layout are often more important than size of print.

■ Check use of ICT (enlarged icons, talking text, teach keyboard skills).

■ Seek advice about low vision aids, special SATs and exam arrangements, etc. from your advisory teacher from the visual impairment service.

■ Do not stand with your back to the window as this creates a silhouette and makes it harder for the pupil to see you

■ Seat the child where there is good lighting – not too bright or too dim.

■ Tell the pupil if there is a change to the layout of a space or any new/temporary obstacles.

■ Point out any objects at head height – wall cupboards, hanging artwork, etc.

■ If you are guiding a student with a visual impairment, let them take your arm or, with a young child, just hold hands. Avoid leaving the child 'in space'; always show them a chair or leave them touching the wall or a piece of furniture.

■ Help pupils to learn frequently used routes, such as classroom-to-toilet. The best route may not be the most direct way, for example a diagonal route across the empty space of a school hall. It's better to trail the walls and be guided by the landmarks passed on the way. A white line painted along the wall at shoulder height can be very helpful.

■ Encourage pupils to learn touch typing and use it use whenever appropriate.

■ Copying from the board or overhead projector may be very difficult, even when the pupil is seated at the front of the class. A clean blackboard or whiteboard helps! Marker pens should not be used when they are running out!

■ Expect the same standards of behaviour, but remember that these pupils may not see well enough to interpret the teacher's gestures or facial expressions. A 'look' may not be sufficient to correct their behaviour.

■ Nominate a work/subject buddy.

Helpful landmarks

All these landmarks can help those with physical or sensory difficulties get around:

■ objects on the wall such as door handles, window ledges, radiators;

■ contrasting colours;

■ textures attached to the wall to show the place where the student might need to cross a corridor;

■ permanently positioned and solid pieces of furniture;

■ changes of surface underfoot, such as gravel and grass, carpet and tiles;

■ contrasting strips along the edge of steps.

Sounds and smells also help, but they may not be there all the time.

Teaching assistants

Teaching assistants (and learning/language support assistants) play an increasingly important role in the inclusion of all pupils within a school. They have a wide range of experience and skills and may have HLTA qualifications. How TAs are managed, however, is often vital to how well they fulfil their function in school.

A survey defined good practice in the work of TAs as:

■ Fostering the participation of pupils in the social and academic processes of a school

■ Seeking to enable pupils to become more independent learners

■ Helping to raise standards of achievement of all pupils.

(Farrell *et al.* 1999)

Teaching assistants can support pupils' participation in classroom activities in a number of ways:

■ helping them to be organised – being prepared for the lesson/homework; planning the work in hand;

■ demonstrating the use of equipment – for example calculators, protractors, compasses, thermometers, scales;

■ reading and interpreting written material and sometimes translating written problems into a format that the child can understand, for example diagrams or physical interpretations of the problems;

■ checking understanding;

■ helping the child to focus on the task;

■ taking notes from the board, noting down homework;

■ supporting pupils in contributing to class discussions. Pupils often like to prepare what they are going to say and validate their responses to an adult before speaking out to the whole class;

- jogging their memory;

- helping children with setting out their work if this aspect holds up the pace of their learning. For example, if the completion of a table of results prevents the child engaging with the real work (the investigation), the teaching assistant could speed up the process by helping to set the table out or providing a template;

- reminding the pupils of the sequence needed to complete the task;

- helping the pupil to find relevant information (and use it effectively);

- helping to catch up with missed work;

- giving encouragement, moral support, and praise.

In supporting the child's social interaction with peers, the teaching assistant should be involved at the planning stage in identifying effective pairs/groups and setting out the objectives for the collaborative work. Turn-taking in speaking and listening may have to be modelled and, in some cases, explicitly taught as part of this process. Outside the classroom, the TA may be involved in coordination of a 'buddy' or 'circle of friends' approach to encourage the inclusion of children socially during breaks and lunchtime.

It is essential that the role of the teaching assistant in the classroom is clearly defined and agreed, so that both teacher and teaching assistant know how each should act in any given situation. Essential aspects of classroom management – such as keeping children on task and spotting early signs of disruption – should be mutually understood and shared. Time is always in short supply, but the work of any teaching assistant will be far more effective if the teacher can spend a few minutes every day/week planning and evaluating. At the very least, the teaching assistant should know what needs to be achieved in a lesson, and what that achievement should look like. Without this guidance, teaching assistants are left to pick up the ideas as best they can, and their interpretations of a task may differ from the teacher's intentions, through no fault of their own.

Effectiveness review for teaching assistants

Teaching assistants can review how they feel about their own effectiveness by asking:

- Do I feel valued as a member of an inclusive learning team?

- Am I clear about my role?

- Are the teachers clear about my role?

- Do I receive appropriate support and feedback from the INCO/SENco?

- Do the teachers involve me in planning and lesson evaluation?

- Do I contribute to reviews of IEPs and annual review meetings?

- Are there opportunities to meet with the INCO/SENco and other teaching assistants to discuss pupil progress, share good ideas and identify CPD requirements?

In some cases, a teaching assistant or learning support assistant will be employed for the benefit of one child, usually by means of a Statement of Special Educational Needs. The teaching assistant may know the child very well and be able to provide the teacher with valuable information on how to meet their learning needs. However, this situation can also lead to the child coming to depend on the teaching assistant, a situation that can impede the development of independence. Teachers need to be aware of this and be able to 'unstick' the pupil from the teaching assistant if necessary.

TAs should avoid . . .	and instead . . .
sitting next to one pupil all the time	work with other pupils, while keeping an eye on the child you are assigned to
staying too close at breaks and lunchtimes	encourage playing with peers, introduce games to include others
collecting/putting away equipment for the child	encourage pupil to do this – with help if necessary
completing a task for the pupil	help the teacher to plan work that is achievable for the child – with minimal support (note down any support given)
allowing behaviour that is either not age appropriate (for example a 10-year-old holding hands), or otherwise unacceptable	encourage the development of more age-appropriate peer relationships through buddying or circle of friends; remind the child of school/classroom rules
making unnecessary allowances, or unrealistic demands	know what the child can do and encourage them to persevere with a task if it is appropriate
preventing a pupil from facing the consequences of their actions	insist that the pupil takes responsibility for their actions
making decisions for the pupil	give the child opportunities to make choices and decisions
speaking for the child	encourage the pupil to ask and answer questions, take part in discussions and plenaries, etc. This may be facilitated by a little careful preparation, or the use of answer cards, symbols, etc.
fostering dependency	encourage the child to do as much as they can by themselves

(Amended from Hull Learning Services 2004)

Bibliography

Booth, T. and Ainscow, M. (2000) *The index for inclusion: Developing learning and participation in schools*, Bristol: Centre for Studies on Inclusive Education.

Briggs, S. (2005) *Inclusion and how to do it: Meeting SEN in primary classrooms*, London: David Fulton Publishers.

Byers, R. and Rose, R. (2004) *Planning the curriculum for pupils with special educational needs*, 2nd edn., London: David Fulton Publishers.

Cheminais, R. (2004) *How to create the inclusive classroom*, London: David Fulton Publishers.

Craig, P. (2006) 'Offering the olive branch', *Special!*, spring.

Datta, J. and Ryder, N. (2005) *Meeting medical needs in mainstream education*, London: NCB.

Davis, P. (2003) *Including children with visual impairment in mainstream schools*, London: David Fulton Publishers.

DfES (Department for Education and Skills) (2000) *Education of children and young people in public care*, London: DfES.

—— (2001a) *Inclusive schooling governors information sheet*, London: DfES.

—— (2001b) *SEN code of practice and SEN toolkit* provides practical advice on carrying out statutory duties to identify, assess and make

provision for children's special educational needs. Online. Available at
www.teachernet.gov.uk/sen.

—— (2001c) *Access to education for children and young people with medical needs*, London: DfES.

—— (2002) *Accessible schools: Planning to increase access to schools for disabled pupils*. Online. Available at www.teachernet.gov.uk/docbank/index.cfm?id=2220.

—— (2003) *Every child matters: Change for children* (sets out the Government's vision for children's services). Online. Available at www.everychildmatters.gov.uk.

—— (2004a) *Removing barriers to achievement* (sets out the Government's vision for giving children with special educational needs and disabilities the opportunity to succeed). Online. Available at www.teachernet.gov.uk/sen.

—— (2004b) *Working together: Giving children and young people a say*, London: DfES.

—— (2005a) *Including me: Managing complex health needs in schools and early years settings*, London: Council for Disabled Children/DfES.

—— (2005b) *Managing medicines in schools and early years settings*, London: Department of Health.

—— (2005c) *Supporting looked after learners: A practical guide for school governors*, London: DfES.

East, V. and Evans, L. (2006) *At a glance . . . A quick guide to children's special needs*, London: Continuum.

Farrell, P., Balshaw, M. and Polat, F. (1999) *The management, role and training of learning support assistants*, London: DfES. Online. Available at www.dfes.gov.uk/rsgateway/DB/RRP/u012780/index.shtml.

Faupel, A., Herrick, E. and Sharp, P. (1998) *Anger management*, London: David Fulton Publishers.

Fletcher-Campbell, F., Archer, T. and Tomlinson, K. (2003) *The role of the school in supporting the education of children in public care*, London: DfES

Galvin, P., Miller, A. and Nash, J. (1999) *Developing and revising a whole school behaviour policy*, London: David Fulton Publishers.

Gordon, M. and Williams, A. (2002) *Special educational needs and disability in mainstream schools: A governor's guide*, London: NASEN.

Hannell, G. (2004) *Promoting positive thinking: Building children's self-esteem, confidence and optimism*, London: David Fulton Publishers.

Harris, J. (1995) 'Responding to pupils with severe learning disabilities who present challenging behaviour', *British Journal of Special Education*, 2 (3) pp. 109–115.

Haslam, L., Wilkin, Y. and Kellet, E. (2005) *English as an additional language: Meeting the challenge in the classroom*, London: David Fulton Publishers.

Hull Learning Services (2004) *Supporting children with medical Conditions*, London: David Fulton Publishers.

—— (2005) *Supporting children with behaviour difficulties*, London: David Fulton Publishers.

—— (2005) *Supporting children with speech and language difficulties*, London: David Fulton Publishers.

Kewley, G. (2005) *Attention deficit hyperactivity disorder: What can teachers do?*, 2nd edn, London: David Fulton Publishers.

Long, R. (2005a) *Challenging confrontation*, London: NASEN/David Fulton Publishers.

—— (2005b) *Developing self-esteem through positive entrapment*, London: NASEN/David Fulton Publishers.

—— (2005c) *Supporting pupils with emotional and behavioural difficulties through consistency*, London: NASEN/David Fulton Publishers.

Mathieson, K. and Price, M. (2002) *Better behaviour in classrooms*, London: Routledge Falmer.

McNamara, E. (1999) *Positive pupil management and motivation: A secondary teacher's guide*, London: David Fulton Publishers.

Miller, O. and Ockelford, A. (2005) *Visual needs*, New York: Continuum.

Ofsted (1999) *Raising the attainment of minority ethnic pupils: School and LEA responses*, London: Ofsted.

—— (2000) *Evaluating educational inclusion: Guidance for inspectors*, London: Ofsted.

—— (2004) *Special educational needs and disability: Towards inclusive schools*, London: Ofsted.

Peer, L. (2005) *Glue ear: An essential guide for teachers, parents and health professionals*, London: David Fulton Publishers.

Special Educational Needs and Disability Act (2001) London: HMSO.

Stacey, H. and Robinson, P. (1997) *Let's mediate*, Bristol: Lucky Duck Publishing.

Stobbs, P. and Rieser, R. (2002) *Making it work: Removing disability discrimination. Are you ready?*, London: National Children's Bureau.

Thomas, H. (2006) *Steps in leadership*, London: David Fulton Publishers.

Wallace, B., Maker, J., Cave, D. and Chandler, S. (2004) *Thinking skills and problem-solving – an inclusive approach: A practical guide for teachers in primary schools*, London: David Fulton Publishers.

Resources, support and further information

AbilityNet UK national charity providing assessments and advice about augmentative and alternative communication. www.abilitynet.co.uk/content/factsheets/Factsheets.htm

ACE Centre Advisory Trust ACE (Aiding Communication in Education) provide specialist assessment for pupils with communication difficulties in England and Wales. Their websites provide many useful downloadable resources and information about all the VOCAs supplied and supported in the UK. www.ace-centre.org.uk

Afasic UK charity representing children and young adults with speech and language impairments, and providing information and advice. www.afasic.org.uk

Association of Workers for Children with Emotional and Behavioural Difficulties www.awcebd.co.uk

BECTA British Educational Communications and Technology Agency ensures that technology supports the DfES's objectives and plays a role in the identification of ICT opportunities for special educational needs. www.becta.org.uk

British Association of Teachers of the Deaf
(BATOD) www.batod.org.uk

British Dyslexia Association (BDA) www.bda-dyslexia.org.uk

Communication Aids for Language and Learning (CALL) Centre Scotland-wide remit to provide information and advice, assessments, loans and technical services, and research and development. The website provides information and many useful downloadable resources. http:CALLCENTRESCOTLAND.ORG.UK

Communication Matters National charitable organization providing free information leaflets on AAC. Also runs a national conference annually. www.communicationmatters.org.uk

Crick Software Products to support literacy teaching including '*Clicker*', which allows children to write with whole words, phrases or pictures. www.cricksoft.com.uk

The Down Syndrome Educational Trust www.downsed.org

The Dyspraxia Foundation www.dyspraxiafoundation.org.uk

I CAN National educational charity for children and young people with speech and language difficulties. Involved in the integration of speech and language therapy and education, promoting collaborative practice in all aspects of the management of children and young people with these difficulties. www.ican.org.uk

Inclusive Technology Specialist company producing hardware and software for use by, and with, children with special needs. Also providers of a range of quality products from other companies (including IntelliTools) and comprehensive training. www.inclusive.co.uk

Jessica Kingsley Publishers of a comprehensive range of books on all aspects of ASD. www.jkp.com

Mencap www.mencap.org.uk

The Mental health Foundation   www.mentalhealth.org.uk

National Attention Deficit Disorder Information and Support Service   www.addiss.co.uk

National Autistic Society (NAS)   UK charity concerned with the education of pupils with autism. www.nas.org.uk

Pyramid Educational Consultants UK Ltd   Provides training in PECS (the Picture Exchange Communication System), used mainly with pupils with autism. www.pecs.org.uk

Royal Institute for the Deaf (RNID)   www.rnid.org.uk

Royal National Institute for the Blind (RNIB)   www.rnib.org.uk

Scope   www.scope.org.uk

Scottish Society for Autism   Leading provider of services for people with autism in Scotland. Also facilitates the **Autism Alliance for Scotland**, which includes the leading regional autism support groups across Scotland. www.autism-in-scotland.org.uk

Semerc   Produces a wide range of software and training to support inclusion. Website includes useful SEN glossary. www.semerc.com

Who Cares? Trust   Publish material concerned with the education of looked-after children (planning, moving school, bullying, staying in school and going to university). www.thewhocarestrust.org.uk

Widgit   Producer of comprehensive symbols system. www.widgit.com

Young Minds   Support for children and adolescent mental health. www.youngminds.org.uk

Index